John Andreoni

Going Wild with FordaBirds

Volume One: 1969-1979

A RedBird Publication

To my wife
who for 40 years religiously read, proofed, and filed
every column I ever wrote.
Not bad for someone
who doesn't rank the outdoor world
at the top of her list.

J.A.

ISBN 978-0-578-04105-6

The columns found in this book all appeared in the *Evening Leader,* St. Marys, Ohio from October 1969 to October 1979. Opinions expressed are mine alone. If there ever was an editorial staff, I never heard from it. In my early years, any guidance and criticism I got came from K.C. Geiger, the finest small town editor and journalist that ever lived. I like to think I write the way she wanted me to…minus the grammatical errors, of course.

Cover and Interior Layout by Beth Daniels of 3 Media Press

RedBird Publications, New Bremen, Ohio
Website: fordabirds.com
Contact: john@fordabirds.com
Facebook: Forda Birds

November, 1966

"In the Beginning"

Everything has a beginning, a middle, and an end. My writing career got kick-started when *Reader's Digest* decided to send me a check for $100 in 1966. Evidently, an anecdote I sent to "Humor In Uniform" struck the funny bone of an editor somewhere, and my "professional" writing career was off and running. Of course, over the years, it never got up enough speed to win any major races. I never sold another piece to the *Digest* or any other major publication, for that matter. I did cash checks from a couple of periodicals with national circulations, but the other 200 or so articles I wrote found a home in state and regional magazines. What does this have to do with putting a book together? Not a whole lot. I don't claim to be great writer or even a decent writer. However, I can live with adequate. All I know is that there are over two million published words out there that I have to claim, most of them appearing in newspapers. What effect they had on people, I'll never know. I don't think anyone was ever harmed, although I have taken a shot or two at people who I thought deserved it. All were public figures of some sort.

Now, what about this book? There comes a time when certain things just have to be done. My wife informed me in February 2009 that I had just finished my 2000th newspaper column. Translated, that meant that I have been spreading the name of "Forda Birds" around Auglaize County for 40 years. Longevity doesn't mean a lot, but the more I thought about the time, I realized that we've experienced many changes in the outdoor world, some good, some bad, some unusual, some humorous, some happy, some sad. Regardless, it seemed logical to pull out select columns and offer them as a capsulated history lesson. Of course, everything you read is the way I saw it, so let the reader beware. What is it they say? "Truth is in the eye of the beholder."

The format I'm going to use is simple. I'll select columns I consider significant, preface them with a few choice comments, and then allow you to touch a piece of local history. Of course, the older I get, the more cynical I've become. I like to temper that cynicism with a bit of humor. It's a lot better to laugh about life than cry about it. I haven't mastered that art, but I keep trying.

So, here we go. Enjoy the read, especially since you paid good money to get your hands on this book. And if you don't enjoy, take a walk in the woods. That should make you feel better.

October 14, 1969

"Who the Hell is Forda Birds?"

I had a number of reasons for starting the "Forda Birds" column 40 years ago. I grew up around fishing and hunting. I was leafing through the pages of the outdoor magazines before I started grammar school, and I frequently listened to stories about the outdoors from old-timers who used to come into our candy store and warm their fannies by a pot-bellied stove we had in the back. It was a good life for a kid. Of course, the Miami-Erie Canal basin was in my backyard. It's a St. Marys city parking lot now, but it was my outdoor world when I was growing up, and I wasn't alone.

I got through high school without building a stellar résumé. My mother constantly reminded me that my priorities were misplaced. I disagreed, of course, although she was probably right. My outdoor world did expand, however, as I grew older and got a bit more mobile.

Somehow, I got into college and eventually graduated. I got an education degree, met my wife, and wound up in the military. Those years took me to places where I discovered an entirely different outdoor world. In 1966, I took a teaching job locally and retired in 1993. Throughout that time, I continued my love of the outdoors and spent many hours outside on the hooks and bullets scene.

But, let's get to the "Forda Birds" issue. When I was in college, I had the urge to write for the outdoor magazines I enjoyed reading. I had an obsession with *Field & Stream*, for some odd reason. I bugged them for information, dropped them story ideas, and even begged to become part of their organization. Eventually, I latched on to a mentor who agreed to read my stuff and tell me all he knew about the outdoor writing business. We corresponded for a number of years, and I learned a great deal from the man. I never met him personally. Come to think of it, he might have been working in circulation for all I know. He did tell me one time that a piece I wrote was so bad he had to do a rewrite before he threw it in the garbage. He was right, and the lesson I learned was try to do my best and not to take myself too seriously.

I wanted to join a premier professional outdoor writing organization. I figured to be a big dog, one had to bark with the big dogs. There was a catch, however. They had membership requirements. A person had to write regularly for pay to qualify. The advice I received was to start writing a column for the local newspaper. So, I wrote a couple of samples, went to see K.C. Geiger, and the rest is history.

I didn't have enough nerve to use a by-line. Instead, I came up with the head, "Outdoor Corner with Forda Birds." That's when I first started hearing the question, "Who the hell is Forda Birds?" When I decided to use my own name as a byline, I continued to hear the question but seldom answered it. To set the record straight, it was a name I took off a mailbox I saw near Traverse City, Michigan. A real person or not? I don't have a clue. However, the name has been around here now for some 40 years, so I guess that makes it official. There is a Forda Birds.

What follows is the first Forda Birds column that appeared on October 16, 1969.

Outdoor Corner

By Forda Birds

To a great number of area sportsmen, the opening of the waterfowl season is a mighty important day. I know of at least one calendar that has an X marked through October 21, and it has been like that since the law was announced last summer.

The excitement and anticipation of opening day is rapidly building. Hunters have put the finishing touches on their blinds and have readied their decoys. They've taken an inventory of last year's ammunition and have blown through their callers at least once. Most of them have their favorite scattergun dug out of the closet. Matter of fact, it wouldn't surprise me if all of the hunters have started to feel that perennial itch to go out to their favorite spot on the lake or a freshly picked corn field and enjoy a good hunt.

It's a funny thing about this itch that waterfowl hunters have. Once you get it, you never seem to be able to get rid of it. You can't cure it, you can only relieve it. To those of you who feel it coming on, here's a few suggestions to help ease the discomfort.

You might relieve that itch by polling your rowboat under the overhanging branches of a willow tree into a quiet backwater pool, watching blackbirds wheel and dip in noisy curiosity, hearing fox squirrels hiding in the hickory and scrub oak scold you for the intrusion, starting as a brace of mallards explode from the water and with a whir of beating wings pick a path among the branches.

It might help your malady if you could be somewhere hearing the whistle of wings behind you and looking into the early morning light waiting for it to develop with no other sound to be heard except the wind clawing through the fence row and the sleet and snow hitting your windbreaker.

Watching flights of blacks and greenheads going out to feed sometimes giving you a pass or two, would help you forget your problem. You would be guaranteed complete relief when that one bunch finally swings your direction and glides slowly into your decoys with wings hooked.

Remember the last time you heard the call of the Canadian Honkers or the higher pitched call of the Blues and Snows? Your itch didn't bother you then. Their cry was very faint yet clearly audible, and you strained your eyes searching for the source of the sound.

As soon as you saw them, they saw your silhouette decoys. As they grew closer, they began their countless circles craning their necks left and right surveying the situation, chuckling their approval at certain shadows and completely ignoring others. You never moved a muscle. Finally they came in low, wings set and the wild birds became unaware of everything around except the food below.

No, the itch old Mother Nature gave waterfowl hunters is enjoyable and they cherish every moment it bothers them. It makes no difference what particular itch the waterfowl season gives you, it won't be too long now before you'll be able to scratch it.

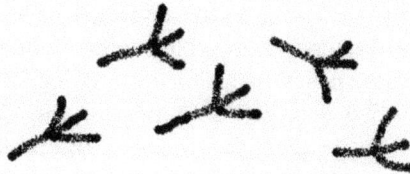

November 22, 1969

"On a Mission"

I've been asked a number of times how I keep coming up with new column ideas every week. For the most part, situations provide the ideas. If an issue comes up and I consider it to have some importance, I'm ready, willing, and able to say my piece. Sometimes, I'm accused of dredging up old columns and simply bringing them up to date. If I do, it's never intentional. Some ideas are seasonal, which means I'll write something about them every year. Other ideas are called "evergreens." That means they can be used when ideas are hard to come by. In October, I'll start writing about waterfowl. Some of my readers think I use the topic too much. In November, I'll spend a couple of weeks on deer hunting, and in April, it's time to hunt turkey. Anyhow, you get the picture. Between seasons, when people are sitting in front of a fire getting warm and waiting for spring fishing, I'll suggest they hit a sport show, and if all else fails, prepare yourself for a column on inside composting.

I was brought up in a hunting and fishing family. At an early age, I was taught to distinguish between right and wrong. That doesn't mean I always followed the "chosen path." As a matter of fact, I have always been a person who tested the waters. My dad always told me that I knew where the line was and not to cross it. More times than not, my toe inched toward the line. On rare occasion, I crossed that barrier and spent an inordinate amount of time going on a guilt trip. Other than that, a lack of nerve had a lot to do with keeping me on the straight and narrow. When it came to the outdoors, however, I didn't have any problem taking a stand.

The first few weeks of "Outdoor Corner", I had little trouble coming up with topics to write about. Things went on in the great outdoors that I didn't like. I jumped on these discretions with abandon. I hit trespassers hard. I jumped on the improper use of pesticides. Slob hunters were next on my agenda. Then, as I really began to feel my oats, I attacked the "American Way." What followed was a column called "Progress and Conservation." If read carefully, it was a pretty gutsy piece. I had no reservations writing it. After all,

7

my by-line didn't appear. If you didn't like what you read, and some local land developers didn't, blame it on Forda Birds.

Outdoors with Forda Birds

"Progress and Conservation"

There is probably more history etched on the nation's landscape than can be found in history books or Congressional Record. In spite of bloodshed and conquest, the Spaniards left a legacy of romance and an easy way of life throughout the Southwest that still prevails. The French, using the many water ways piercing the Continent, were aware of the greatness and excitement of their travels and created an atmosphere that still lingers. The English, a little less romantic, pushed their frontier West with the practical eye for land occupancy and a stubbornness that excelled all others. One characteristic common to all of these nations was the raw courage of conquest. These adventurers came from all points of the compass and probed a wilderness that had no dimensions. They had no master plan in the conquest of our Continent but, accidentally, their efforts laid the foundation of a mighty nation.

The old Colonists felt the full impact of the massive forests, serene, primitive, and dangerous. Like the space travelers of today, they took a challenge and began westward migration and settlement. The wilds became both their enemy and their friend; and there followed much thoughtless cutting and burning from the Atlantic to the Mississippi. These dots of human activity were the beginning of a future civilization, and the migration from the eastern seaboard is more truly representative of the nation's history.

Our whole history was very different from the old feudal systems of Europe. The breed of people in our country wanted and got absolute control and title of great expanses of land. At an early date this concept of individual, absolute land control caused some concern. In the 19th Century a European traveler observed: "In America there is no sovereign right over forests and game, no forest service. Whoever holds new land, in whatever way, controls it as his exclusive possession, with everything on it, above it, and under it. It will not easily come about therefore that, as a strict statutory matter, farmers and landowners will be taught how to manage their forests so as to leave for their grandchildren a bit of wood over which to hang a kettle." The rule of the land used by the settler was really very simple—try it and see what the land will do.

This, in a nutshell, is the history of American land development. In the beginning there was so much for so few that planning seemed unnecessary. But, by the time the last frontier was under control, there were already areas from the New England States to the Gulf of Mexico that were worn out and being abandoned. Nature had made an effort to heal the scars of land abuse with coarse grasses and shrubs, and they slowly began the tedious task of regenerating a new forest or a better grassland cover.

The wealth of our natural resources was beyond imagination. It had to be enormous to create our nation and feed much of the underprivileged world. Citizens of the United States have much to be thankful for despite "rural slums"—land gullied by floods, scarred by mechanical monsters, and with streams carrying far too much precious top soil to the Delta.

Because of its resources, because of the nature of the people who invaded it determined to obtain its wealth, the United States today stands as the world's leader. How long can it hold that position? Our few short centuries of progress have brought the average citizen a vote, a bank account, one and a fraction healthy children, a new car, and a high opinion of himself. Progress has not given the average man the ability to live in high density populations without befouling and destroying his environment, nor a belief that such an ability is the true test of being civilized.

Omar Bradley once said, "If we are not careful we shall leave our children a legacy of billion-dollar roads leading nowhere except to other congested places like those left behind.

Our beautiful country is becoming less beautiful. Our indifference is causing this to happen. Our indifference supports the assumption that we are a "chosen people", and that assumption no longer holds any water. It is a most frightening attitude and could lead us down the road of self destruction.

April 11, 1970

"A Lion in Auglaize County"

In late March of 1970, I changed the column name to "Outdoors with Forda Birds" and put my name to it. I'm not too sure why I did that, but the choice was definitely related to the positive response I was getting from the readers. Actually, since there weren't any negative letters to the editor, I figured it was safe to take the blame for whatever I wrote. K.C. Geiger also strongly suggested that it was time to start using my own byline.

By now, I was setting into a pattern. I had gone though my "hot button" issues, and found myself writing pieces about weather lore, map reading, and tree identification. Of course, it was the spring fishing season, and that provided current material. All in all, however, I was scrambling for something to write about, something exciting. Then it happened. Someone spotted a lion roaming around Auglaize County. I was skeptical, to say the least, but when I heard the initial sighting was made by a nun, I had second thoughts. After all, nuns don't go about fabricating stories. That's not a nun thing to do. When other reports started to come in, and someone had seen tracks, I knew that I was dealing with my first big story, and I was going lion hunting.

I began my research in earnest. I called a couple of area hunters who had been on an African safari. One had seen the tracks and swore they were made by a lion. Another said just the opposite. Regardless, I eventually went to the scene and was shown some very large animal prints. I started following them along a ditch bottom until I found myself in the middle of a very large culvert. It suddenly dawned on me that this was an ideal place for the big cat to enjoy a meal. However, I didn't hang around long enough to find out. I made a plaster cast of the print, the animal was never seen again, the African hunters kept arguing who knew the most about big cats, and the nun probably spent the rest of her life regretting she ever mentioned her encounter with the "King of the Jungle."

Outdoors with Forda Birds

"I'm Not Ly'n, I Saw a Lion"

It was interesting to read reports of a possible lion roaming our areas and even more interesting to consider the odds against this event taking place. Most people believe that it is impossible, and my better judgment makes me go along with the majority; yet in our own area, in Pennsylvania, Kentucky, Michigan, and other states close by, sightings of large cats are almost an annual occurrence. I don't know if any of these reports were ever substantiated, but nevertheless something is being seen by people and around here is leaving sizeable tracks.

It is impossible for a 400-600 lb. African lion to be in this area, unless he escaped from captivity; but what are the chances that a smaller cat, such as the cougar, has made his way into the Auglaize County area? This, too, is highly improbable, but I don't believe it's absolutely impossible.

The cougar (mountain lion, puma, panther, and even catamount) was originally found all over the United States. Since this great cat doesn't care to be around man, he left when our population began to grow. The mountain lion has been considered extinct east of the Mississippi for the past 100 years. Moving didn't hurt this animal, because he was and still is very adaptable. He is found today in areas ranging from sea level to 14,000 ft. above sea level. He is a voracious eater, and even though he prefers to feed on deer does not pass up a rabbit or other small animals. When he's hungry, which is almost constantly, he'll eat what is available and even the field mouse is not too small.

The cougar was originally a forest animal and as our forest regions began to vanish, the big cat moved west to areas where man had not yet ventured and is existing there today. His major stomping grounds are the Southwest, the Rockies and Western Canada. There is also a small population found in the swamps of Florida. The cougar is a beautiful animal, swift, powerful, and graceful. He may reach a length of seven feet from his nose to the tip of his tail, and a male will weigh on the average of 80 to 100 lbs. with some weighing as much as 200 lbs. His color varies, and he may be red, brown, gray or black. His ears and the tip of his tail may be dark, his belly white. In normal gait, his distance of pace is around 22 to 24 inches and his paw size averages 4 inches in length and 5 inches in width. When he turns on the speed, this animal is capable of leaps of 20 ft.

I've only had one encounter with this great cat and that was in Kansas a few years ago. He was a rare visitor and obviously unwanted as two bird hunters greeted him with a couple of loads of shot. Concerned that the cat might become a problem if wounded, local conservationists and interested sportsmen decided to track the animal. Dogs were obtained and the chase was on. The cat was tracked for three days, yet we never saw the animal. We did find many signs. A mouse nest was torn apart, a few jackrabbit carcasses were spotted, and in one instance a freshly killed deer was found. The cat was a stranger to Kansas and had somehow strayed into the territory. When man and dog got on his tail, he headed north, and as far as we could determine never stopped.

A big cat in Kansas is very rare, and a big cat in our area is many more times unlikely. Who knows? Maybe a cougar with a poor sense of direction and a desire for adventure has somehow found his way here. If he has, don't worry. This animal doesn't want anything to do with you. He prefers to be left alone and will do his part to make sure that man seldom, if ever, sees him.

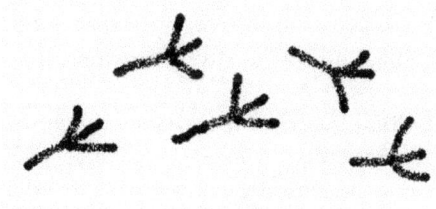

May 9, 1970

"No More Geese in Mercer County"

In the early 1950s, I used to enjoy visiting a couple of ponds located next to State Route 127 just south of Celina. The ponds supported a small resident flock of Canada geese maintained by a fellow named Gilbert. For some odd reason, this collection of birds wasn't very popular with the locals, especially hunters, and Gilbert pulled up stakes after someone supposedly shot out some windows in his house.

Shortly after the Gilbert incident, the Mercer Wildlife Area was formed and dedicated to the establishment of a resident Canada goose flock. Needless to say, the project was a grand success, if you happened to be someone who wanted a lot of geese in the area. For many waterfowl hunters, this was a "no-brainer." There were those, however, who didn't care for the great birds and casually voiced their objections whenever the opportunity arose. Then the proverbial "goose poop" hit the fan. So happy with their success, the Division of Wildlife thought it would be a great idea to expand the refuge and increase the local goose population. True or not, a property owner close to the refuge was queried about the possible sale of his farm for "goose roost" expansion. What went on in that meeting is only known by those in attendance, but the reports that made it to the public threw Mercer County into turmoil.

The story that started floating around was that somewhere during the conversation the threat of eminent domain came up. The farmer might as well sell because the state would get the property one way or another. Now, I don't know whether this threat was ever made, but if a certain Division of Wildlife big shot I met was involved, it wouldn't have surprised me. He was a loud-mouth bully, plain and simple, or at least tried to be. Shortly after writing the column you're about to read, this character pulled me aside at a meeting and told me that I wasn't to write anything more about the subject unless he read it first and approved it. I was new to the game and really didn't know what to say. Instead, I wrote pieces in July and September, without his okey-dokey.

13

In the long run, the goose refuge never expanded, the MRZ zone died a natural death, and today, the Canada goose is considered a nuisance by some and a trophy by others. I guess the choice is determined by the amount of "goose poop" you have in your lawn.

Outdoors with Forda Birds

"There's Going to be Bloodshed"

"Friends, we've got trouble right here in River City." This is probably one of the most famous lines from the musical, *Music Man*. Well, friends, we've got trouble around Lake St. Marys, and that starts with T, and that rhymes with G, and that stands for Goose.

A person can almost feel the change in temperature as he drives into Mercer County. It's hotter there because of anger, anger brought on by two factors: the proposed expansion of the Mercer County Waterfowl Refuge and the new law controlling goose hunting within a 10 mile radius of the refuge. I've been following this situation ever since it began to develop and have shied away from talking about it because a number of emotionally distraught people have been camouflaging the truth with questionable statistics, loaded words, and highly charged statements. Make no mistake, this column is basically nothing more than the opinion or conclusion of one person, an opinion or conclusion which must be logically drawn based on facts. I don't have any set opinions on this matter because concrete information is impossible to obtain from this big, "can of worms". I do have questions, lots of questions for both the Columbus "Tower of Power" and the Mercer County people that have thrown good judgment to the wind. My problem is that I don't have many answers.

The Mercer County people I know, mostly farm people, are very independent, self-reliant, honest, practical, rational, God-fearing men, and I carry a great deal of admiration and respect for them. I have absolutely no use, however, for people who make statements such as this one that appeared in the Celina Daily Standard. "I hate to see my friends' lands grabbed from under them. The state could care less about these families. If the state (meaning game wardens also) keep up their pace, there is going to be bloodshed and the raising of voices. If I were a game warden, I would think twice before taking any action on these matters." Talking about bloodshed seems to me to be pretty

14

loose talk for someone who is not directly affected by the problem, or any one for that matter. The property owners themselves are the group that stands to be affected and if they feel that their way of life is being threatened, they should stand up and be heard. Of course, when there's a battle to be fought, every Tom, Dick, and Harry has to hop on the band wagon and sound off. The majority of these people may be sincere in helping their fellow man, but I question the motives of some.

Why doesn't the Concerned Property Owners Association (CPOA) simply say that they don't want to give up their homes because their homes are their lives? I respect their belief. But no, some individuals either within the CPOA, but more likely outside the organization, are weakening their arguments by cramming a pile of unproven, invalid figures into the minds of the people of Mercer County and by using faulty logic are building a defense that could be torn apart by any first year law student. Yes, Mercer County is over reacting at the present time. They've pushed the panic button. A state man talks to a property owner about selling his property for refuge expansion and immediately someone comes up with the term, power of eminent domain. By the time word gets around, rumors have it that Joe Blow down the road has been ordered from his land by January 1971. From information I have been able to pick up, no one can actually say they were threatened by the State of Ohio and further information shows that the Division of Wildlife has rarely exercised this power of eminent domain.

Somebody says that the state is talking about 200,000 geese. Any person, especially a farmer, should know that a piece of land has a certain carrying capacity. But no, people have seen the problems that are created by the 6000 resident birds and when they multiply those problems by 30+, they panic and see 200,000 geese raping their land and their families neck deep in goose manure. The entire goose population of the Tennessee Flyway is about 105,000 birds and authorities throughout Ontario, Michigan, Ohio, Kentucky, Tennessee, and Alabama would like to see it increased to around 150,000. These birds pass through the entire state and at the Mercer County Refuge a maximum of only 16,000 birds have remained at one time. From what I understand, the purpose of expansion is to hold more birds during the fall migration, not to increase the resident flock.

Another statement that has been tossed around is that geese are polluting the lake and that two geese equal one human in the amount of pollution they create. This statement is too vague for me to buy. For example, from reading I have done, I have found that bacteria in goose waste is not readily comparable to the bacteria in human waste. Human waste contains many more bacteria that are harmful to man. I agree that some pollution may exist, but again, the amount of pollution can only be shown by study and analysis. Another question I need answered is the sudden concern about goose pollution. It seems to me that pollution caused by the inadequate sewage systems along the lake shores and the gas and oil from the thousands of power boats that run around the lake are just as important. Why hasn't anyone jumped on that? Evidently, since only goose pollution is a popular gripe, the rest is to be ignored. Right now, people are using their logic to arrive at the conclusion that the 200,000 geese the state is talking about is the same thing as having 100,000 people using Lake St. Marys as their personal bathroom. If this were true, people should react. But is it?

Tax loss from property purchased by the state has been mentioned as a problem. Yes, there probably would be some tax loss, and this loss would have to be made up by the property owner, every property owner in the county. The property valuation of Mercer County is $136,849,809.00. If the county wanted to replace the money lost from this property, what amount of millage would have to be added to the present tax load? Not very much by my figures. However, any tax increase is hard to swallow. And what about the increased revenue being brought into Mercer County by the visiting hunter? It has been estimated that each goose killed brings between $76 and $100 into the area. It seems to me that a development in sport attractions would bring in more people and therefore bring in revenue more than covering any tax loss.

Concern is shown for pilots using the Lakefield Airport. I don't question the possibility that danger exists, but not being a flyer, I don't know how great it is.

If you've read this far, you've probably convinced yourself that I am part of this "great goose conspiracy" and am expecting to be rewarded by those in favor of the proposal and law. Guess again. My views, unclear at the moment, are my own and they're not for sale. I've taken a great deal of time discussing the Mercer Countian viewpoint because right now they are making the most noise,

As for the state, they are making very little noise. I believe that the state personnel at the waterfowl refuge are doing their job well, maybe too well. Geese are their business and the increase in birds over the years is proof of their dedication, I also believe that the game protectors (not game wardens) are doing a great public service and should not be held in contempt because they work for the state. As for the state officials in Columbus, I can't definitely say but it seems to me that a certain degree of bureaucracy exists. There appears to be people in Columbus who pursue a narrow routine, following rigid and formal measures, thriving on red tape and ignoring the common people such as the Mercer County people. This is evident to me because of the lack of communications between the people and the state offices. Public relations to the state seems unimportant, and this is shown by their neglect in not informing the Mercer and Auglaize County people of their plans.

The lack of courtesy that was shown to Mercer County people is, to me, inexcusable and the people responsible are bordering on incompetence. Common sense would tell a person that people living in a democracy don't particularly care to have laws and proposals jammed down their throats. It makes no difference if it is good or bad, people won't swallow it. I mentioned the word courtesy. I hope that the officials in Columbus see a need for working together with the people they serve. If they don't, any change brought about in the future will be fought tooth and nail. My recommendations to the State of Ohio are to hire some good public relations people to let us know what's going on before it happens; and if they have public relations people now, get rid of them. They aren't doing their job. It may also help keep situations like the one in Mercer and Auglaize County from developing if someone climbs down from his Columbus perch and sees how the other half lives.

I've been throwing stones since the beginning of this column, but they weren't thrown in anger. They were thrown to wake people and get them to use their heads. To the majority of you readers, my purpose was simply to inform you of a miserable condition that now exists west of us.

Every waterfowl hunter should now be aware of the 10 mile law, and since I've commented on the refuge expansion proposal, a few words on this law are in order. The law to me was made with good intentions. The law that came out is a different kettle of fish. In a state as populated as ours, a certain amount of control must be placed on the waterfowl hunter by someone. It should be a control that benefits the majority of hunters and hinders that majority that violates the rights of property owners and sportsmen alike. The state has justified this law by saying that they are preventing the Federal government from taking control of our waterfowl hunting. This may be, and I personally wouldn't care to see our area run like Wisconsin's Horicon Marsh or Illinois' Horseshoe Lake-Union County Areas. I also see that this law could give the Mercer and Auglaize County farmer more hunter control of his land.

The law, as I interpret it, also has its bad points. Our area is basically a duck area and the goose that a hunter bags is a bonus bird. By restricting goose hunting, you also restrict duck hunting. A $10 permit is to be obtained by any farmer if he allows goose hunting on his land. They are also obligated to keep a record of all birds killed. To me, this is fine if the farmer charges to hunt. If the farmer doesn't wish to charge, the $10 fee is ridiculous. Many farmers have shared their land with hunters for years, and many grand friendships have developed. Why should a man have to pay a fee for having friends? This mandatory fee is bringing forced commercialization. Commercialization of waterfowl hunting will not benefit this area, and many farmers will not give up friendships for a few dollars or obligate themselves by leasing or renting their land to certain individuals. As it stands now, many farmers south of the lake will not obtain a goose permit this fall. Some are closing their property to waterfowl hunting altogether. Those who do obtain permits and begin to charge hunters for hunting geese will also charge for hunting ducks. These attitudes create a great number of limitations for the hunter to overcome. Some control is necessary, but I believe that the restrictions placed on the landowner, as well as the hunter, are a slight bit unreasonable. I think the 10 mile law would be easier to swallow if the owner who did not charge hunters would not be required to pay the fee. This part of the law could be changed with no problem and should be changed now.

I hesitate to predict the future of the Mercer County Waterfowl refuge. Somebody should start identifying some values and determine the importance of our waterfowl program. In this century, man will either guarantee his survival or insure his destruction. Can geese and man live in harmony on Lake St. Marys? I don't know. Will fathers be able to pass down to their sons any type of natural heritage? I don't know. I do know that I would hate to see the day that the wild goose could only be found in a picture book and the right for a man to own property no longer existed. Only time will tell what the future holds.

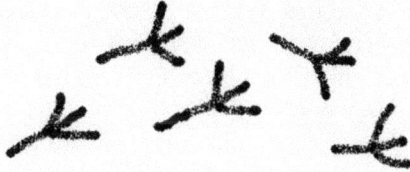

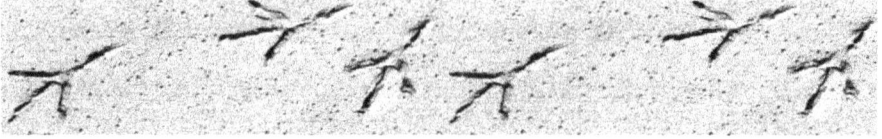

November 21, 1970

The Pheasant Depression

In the 1940s, when I first started playing dog for my dad, there were quite a few pheasants roaming the area. Of course, the numbers never equaled those found in counties further north, but flushing a big rooster or two during the season was expected. If one happened to have the services of a good dog, the probability increased dramatically.

There might have been a few good purebred bird dogs in the county, but I never knew anyone who owned one. Then there was Ginger, our family mutt. My sister brought her back from a trip she made to visit our Kentucky relatives. My dad and mom wanted nothing to do with this little puppy, but eventually gave in to my sister's whining. Actually, that isn't fair. My sister seldom whined. She was much more calculating than that. If I remember correctly, she pointed out to my dad that the dog was part beagle. One could tell by the white tipped tail, she said. My dad, who loved the hounds, bought her story, and Ginger had a home. I still don't know why he ignored the black longitudinal stripes that ran the length of the dog's body. To me, Ginger always looked like she was part raccoon, but who cared what I thought. Besides, she was my sister's dog, and I had no attachment to it.

Well, the dog lost his white-tipped tail, my sister lost interest, and Ginger and I became close friends. Then, when Ginger was a little over a year old, my dad decided to take her along rabbit hunting. Our Kentucky mutt turned out to be a fabulous hunting dog. She had an outstanding nose, was faster than blazes, found rabbits almost at will, and went ballistic whenever she got around a pheasant. If the dog came upon a bird, she would begin to shake uncontrollably. That was the time to get ready. Once the dog focused on the bird, she would charge into any cover the bird happened to be hiding in and flush it. As far as I know, she never ran by a bird and for a number of years produced some exciting times for us in the field.

Ginger died while I was in Vietnam, and my mother didn't tell me until I returned home. I think she was 16 at the time. Regardless, my first dog was now a pleasant memory, and so were the pheasants in Auglaize County. By the time I returned home, these great sporting birds were gone.

Outdoors with Forda Birds

"You can't shoot 'em out!"

I think that any upland game hunter would agree that we're in the middle of pheasant depression. The factors that cause the bottom to fall out of the ring-neck population, from time to time, are as much a mystery to wildlife biologists as they are to the thousands of hunters that seek this elusive, trophy bird.

Since nothing concrete can be presented as proof, everybody and his brother is given the "go-ahead" to contrive a pet theory and throw it in the pot of knowledge where it is mixed with other theories until each factual statement is falling off the bones. When it is recognized that a problem exists, people just grab into the pot, pull out, and follow any bit of information that they get their hands on. Let's take a look at a few scraps that are floating around in the soup.

Pheasants have a formidable list of enemies: If the opportunity presents itself, almost any meat-eating creature will dine on pheasant. Fortunately, those opportunities don't happen very often, because if they did, the foxes, mink, raccoon, weasels, cats, dogs, great horned owls, Cooper's hawks, red-tailed hawks, skunks, opossums, crows, rats and snakes would soon eliminate, at some time during the year, every adult bird, chick, and egg in a given area. The pheasant population is not like your bank account. If you take a dollar out there is one less and the other dollars cannot reproduce it. Nature has given wildlife the ability to reproduce in large numbers to replace their losses. Even though the predators destroy a number of birds every year, they are by no means capable of total destruction.

Hunting pressure has destroyed pheasant population: One of the surest things that wildlife people know is that, "You can't shoot 'em out!" The age-old law of diminishing returns is responsible for this. As roosters are shot, the remaining ones get harder and harder to find. As they get harder to find, hunters begin to lose interest and are much less successful.

Let's say, for example, that an area has one cock pheasant and three hens. Taking into consideration natural factors, this family should produce nine cocks and nine hens. Even if 90 percent of the cocks were harvested by hunters, that one remaining bird would be enough to provide an adequate breeding combination for good fertility. If one stops to think a bit, the importance of saving hens is obvious.

Stock more birds; you'll have more birds: Sportsman Associations and the state tend to believe in this philosophy; but to me, it is a waste of time and money. Pheasants are a crop of the land, and I think that any farmer will agree that you can't increase yield just by seeding heavier.

I've heard two sides to this story. The manager of the Sun Enterprise Game Farm, one of the largest in the world, told me that approximately 65 percent of the birds he released were harvested. I've seen his records, and he is the first to admit that releasing birds on the morning of the hunt, turning them loose in isolated cover, and using well trained bird dogs, have a great deal to do with his success.

Dr. Bob Robel, a wildlife biologist that used to work for the Michigan Game Division, ran a study a number of years ago on birds that were released as soon as they were able to leave fly pens. The release time was a number of weeks before the hunting season, and his records show that less than one-half of one percent were harvested by hunters. I wonder how many of the pheasants that were released in this area will be harvested. I'll bet not many; and I'm positive that the number of birds taken would never justify such a release program.

Herbicides and pesticides are destroying our pheasant population: This is an interesting theory and I'm sure that pheasants are being killed in significant numbers by these poisons. However, I would have to question any statement that blamed these poisons as the main cause of the pheasant shortage. It has been shown that these birds can handle a much greater amount of certain poisons than man, but this does not take into consideration that a bird's high metabolic rate causes him to consume food constantly to stay alive. A young pheasant chick's initial diet consists of insects, and they are bound to consume enough poison in this food chain to create a significant mortality rate. However, weed control, poor drainage, mechanized equipment, fall plowing, and burning, would also have a significant effect on a pheasant's existence.

All of the factors that I've mentioned have caused a depletion of our pheasant population, but not one of these alone is the guilty party. To me, the guilty party is man. That's right, our society and its values have destroyed the pheasants around here. The value of the dollar, Jack; that's what has eliminated the birds. A pheasant needs fertile soil, which he has. He also needs food and shelter, properly distributed, which he doesn't have; as well as certain types of the same food and shelter which is lacking. Take away any of these and you eliminate pheasants.

Take a look at the farms in this area. Granted, there are some cover areas, but look at the amount of land that is clean farmed, the number of fence rows that are as bare as a new baby's bottom, and the ditches that are stripped of all cover. That land won't hold birds. Is the farmer to blame? Absolutely not. He has to harvest maximum yield from his land to compete in the economy. In doing this, he sacrifices habitat for wildlife. The farmer has to make the choice, and the choice is obvious because a large population of pheasants won't pay the light bill.

What I've stated is theory not fact. But, I'd love to see the Moulton Gun Club, Western Ohio Fish and Game, and the Mercer County Sportsman Association, take an area of land, develop it according to professional guidelines, and prove that I'm wrong. I might be, but the results of that type of problem would be much more valuable than turning loose pheasants every year.

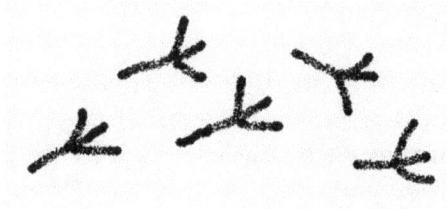

January 23, 1971

The Cagey Coyote

I enjoyed writing about unique wildlife visitors to Ohio's outdoors. On occasion, a bear would cross over from Pennsylvania or West Virginia and create quite a stir. Another rarity made its mark when the cagey coyote showed up in southwestern Ohio. Although there had been scattered sightings over the years, no one gave them a second thought, not even the wildlife management people. In the fall of 1970, two of these animals were killed by bird hunters, and I reacted by saying that even the coyote had a place in the wilds of Ohio. It was the "live and let live philosophy" that I went by, and it's still the one I prefer today. After all, what impact would a couple of coyotes have on the outdoor grand scheme of things? Little did I realize that almost four decades later thousands of the animals would be roaming Ohio. Human population growth and urban sprawl didn't seem to be the formula for a coyote boom. No doubt the animals are adaptive, and it appears they're here to say. If their population continues to grow along with their demand for food, I wonder what the response will be from people when they start losing their family pets to a hungry coyote. Even more, heaven forbid, a small child, although that seems unlikely. It seems to me that if I had property and someone wanted to hunt coyotes, I'd be inclined to let them. Now, there's a change of heart.

Outdoors with Forda Birds

"Control, yes—extermination, no."

Ask almost anyone what a coyote is and he'll probably tell you that it's a dumb wild dog that spends all day chasing road-runners (which it never catches) and all night howling at the moon. He'll go on to tell you that this animal lives in the West, can most frequently be seen when Roy Rogers and the Sons of the Pioneers sing sweet melodies to a herd of cattle, and is constantly being imitated by blood-thirsty Indians as they approach Jimmy Stewart who knows that the howls he hears are really signals marking his downfall. Thanks to Hollywood and the Saturday morning cartoons, most of us will agree. Well, we're wrong because the coyote (ki-o-tee) (ki-oat) is probably one of the smartest, far-ranging animals roaming our country today.

The original range of the coyote was prairie country and they thrived on the kills of the grizzly bear and the big gray wolf as these killers fed on the buffalo, deer, and elk that abounded in the virgin grass country. The coyote killed some of their own meat of the lesser species, from jackrabbits and prairie dogs down to occasional gophers and mice. But, if they wanted to feast on deer, elk, antelope, or buffalo, they usually sat back until the big boys were finished and then scavenged what was left.

The primitive conditions have long passed. Comparatively speaking, a few mule deer and antelope remain and the "great" herds of buffalo now roam federal game refuges and some private ranches. Elk have moved to the mountains further west and gray wolves and grizzly bears are rarely seen anywhere between Canada and Mexico. With the coming of man and the disappearance of the large predators, the coyote was forced to fend for himself and out of necessity extended his primitive-day range to a truly remarkable degree. They're now found far up in Canada, clear into Alaska, and are locally numerous in Mexico. The coyote ranges east covering all of Michigan, the western edge of Ohio, all of Indiana, the western half of Arkansas, and all but the extreme eastern edge of Texas.

It's hard to believer that coyotes exist in Ohio, but a few are seen every year and occasionally one is bagged by a varmint hunter in the field. As a matter of fact, two coyotes were reported taken during the upland game season in the southwest corner of Ohio, one by a 14 year old boy from Hamilton and

24

another by a fellow from Miamisburg. The coyotes were killed in Butler and Warren Counties, according to the Ohio Division of Wildlife.

Since the range of this predator has changed so drastically in the past 150 years, his nature and food habits have also been forced to change just as sharply. He is still a slinking and cowardly member of the wolf clan in his dealings with man, but that's just his extreme intelligence showing. Hunters and trappers have hounded him for years, and now he knows that human scent means death and the unseen coyote has the longest life expectancy.

According to studies made in Kansas, rabbits make up 53 percent of the coyote's diet. Carrion account for 27 percent, chickens 7.3 percent, rodents 7.7 percent and other mammals, wild birds, game girds, fruits, berries, grain and others make up the difference. A coyote requires 1 ½ pounds of meat a day and according to the studies, this would mean that the minimum annual requirement for the coyote would be approximately 140 rabbits. The figures are deceiving, however, since availability of food determines the variety.

Since the coyote has such a voracious appetite, man has classified him as a predator and has dedicated himself to this animal's destruction. To me, destruction of this species is questionable. Any predator helps to maintain a natural balance. Kansas states that 53 percent of the coyote's diet is rabbit, while Oregon, California, Colorado and Wyoming are refusing help from the Predatory Animal Control people because they are concerned with the vast plant damage caused by an over abundance of rodents. Evidently, man must learn to see the complete picture before he acts.

Regardless of his questionable personal qualities, the coyote can and should have a place in our environment. Control, yes—extermination, no. If the old coyote was no longer around, how do you think Hollywood, cowboys, Indians, and the road runners would feel? They'd miss him dearly.

February 6, 1971

Sunday Hunting

As I began to work my way through 40 years of columns trying to select the most significant, the Sunday hunting controversy seemed to fit the bill. That's right; there was a time when Sunday hunting wasn't allowed. As a matter of fact, although it had been brought up before on more than one occasion, allowing hunters to hit the field on the Sabbath was never given any serious consideration.

Of course, I chose to address the issue because like many hunters, I worked five days a week and only had one day free to hunt. In a personal note, since I enjoyed waterfowl hunting, more often than not, Sunday seemed to produce nastier weather than Saturday, and foul weather moved the birds. It was frustrating to see ducks fly on Sunday and soak up the sun on Saturday.

I knew the main resistance would come from the various religions, their ministers and the faithful, but right was right, and logic was logic. After all, at the time, 38 other states had Sunday hunting, and every other outdoor sport seemed to be permitted on the Seventh Day. I never understood why a golfer could have an early Sunday morning tee time, and I couldn't be sitting in a duck blind at the same time.

Regardless, I set myself up for inevitable repercussions if I wrote about the subject. My mother was horrified that I would question any church teachings, and my father stayed out of the discussion. After careful consideration and a rudimentary search of the Good Book where I found no mention of Sunday hunting, I decided to take the plunge and tackle what I thought was an antiquated rule.

It took awhile, but Sunday hunting finally made it on the books. I don't think anyone really suffered from the change.

Outdoors with Forda Birds

Legalize Sunday Hunting: Why Not?

February is nature's "half-time," and thousands of sportsmen spend much of it sitting in front of the fire waiting for the game to begin again in the spring. At the same time, some men plod on following the same foot trodden path they've been using for years. Governmental agencies and private organizations are preparing a meal of propaganda for us to swallow with a big serving of statistics for dessert. The county has already wasted $300 by paying bounties, and individuals who have spent the past few months condemning all hunters and all hunting (except during election time) are desperately seeking a new cause to support or tear apart.

I can't do much for the government agencies or the private organizations. It's too late for the county to do anything about their annual bounty "boo-boo". But I can help the crusader by giving him a new band wagon to ride. I don't know how much good it will do because many of the crusaders I know are as neurotic as my bird dog and are as objective in their thinking as a man that plants sod with the green side down. Some crusaders, however, are intelligent and analytical—we need them. Regardless of their qualifications, I love them all and every once in awhile pick up some good points from their desperate bantering.

If my crusading friends disagree, please don't come back with anything as trite as, "People in glass houses shouldn't throw stones." Try something a little less common like, "Blessed are they who have nothing to say and cannot be persuaded to say it", or "Wise men talk because they have something to say; fools because they have to say something."

What's the band-wagon I'm giving away? It's simply doing away with an archaic law and legalizing Sunday hunting in Ohio the same as in 38 other states. This action has been attempted before, and another effort will be made this year to change the present law. The movement will be headed by State Rep. David E. Armbruster of Butler County.

Advocates of Sunday hunting point out that a majority of Ohio sportsmen are unable to take time off from work during the week and consequently are denied to hunt on their weekend free time. They also feel that there is no difference between their sport and boating, fishing, golf, camping, etc., all of which are permitted in Ohio.

Major opposition, according to reports from the Middletown area, has come from clergymen across the state who believe that permitting Sunday hunting would cut down the attendance during hunting season. It seems to me that if this were true, one of two things should take place. Clergymen should be fighting to outlaw all Sunday sports or clergymen should examine their product and try to figure out why they are so afraid that what they have to offer will play second fiddle to a nine-iron, spinning rod, or shotgun, for that matter.

Clergymen have no objections to this bill, however, because it will only ask for hunting on Sunday afternoons. Rep. Armbruster's bill will give the Ohio hunter a choice of an additional half-day of hunting or a continuation of the total Sunday hunting ban. To me, a half-day of Sunday hunting is a compromise that the sportsmen of Ohio shouldn't buy. The ¾ of a million hunters in this state should let themselves be heard by writing their state officials and informing them of the fact that they are being discriminated against by law.

There are other factors to consider in legalizing Sunday hunting such as game population and game management practices. If a day of rest is conducive to good game management, I don't think the game would mind having it on a weekday while the hunter is on the job.

A small stone should be thrown at the Sunday hunting opposition, but a rock should be pitched directly at the law, a law that should be taken from the books. The attitude seems to be that once a law is written, it should never be changed. This attitude is nonsense and has created a number of nonsense laws that are still in effect today. The ban on Sunday hunting is one of them.

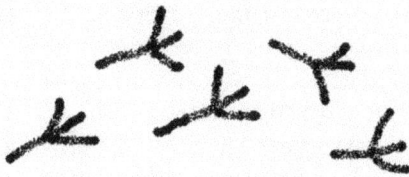

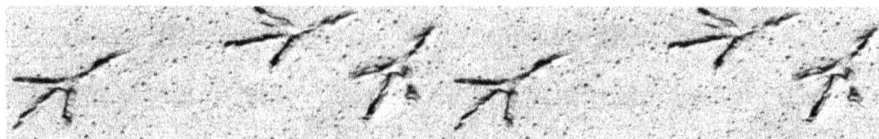

June 26, 1971

From Pensacola, Florida

I joined the Outdoor Writers Association of America in 1969. From what I had been told, it was a premier organization comprised of the big-name outdoor communicators from around the country. Since I had it in the back of my mind to make outdoor writing my career, it made perfectly good sense to hang with the big guns. Besides, I qualified as a card carrying member, albeit by the skin of my teeth.

Over the years, I attended various annual meetings and met a lot of big-name people. I had the opportunity to interview, question, or just share a drink with many of them. In the outdoor communication arena, Hurley Campbell, Clare Conley, Grits Gresham, Lou Klewer, Wally Taber, Curt Gowdy, and Homer Circle come to mind. Government officials made their appearances with great regularity. What better way to get out a message, promote an agenda, or cover one's butt than to hobnob with the outdoor press. I think I met at least four different Secretaries of the Interior at various meetings I attended and scads of other officials. Of course, James Watt was the most memorable Interior Secretary to attend an OWAA meeting since no one in the outdoor world trusted him. Many referred to him as, "a fox in the hen house." Come to think of it, as a token of appreciation for his appearance, the organization presented him a beautifully mounted stuffed fox instead of a plaque.

I admit that I was in awe as I got the chance to rub elbows with these "big guns." They were all excellent communicators, and I took every word they said as the gospel truth. Then, at a meeting in Florida, I met the first head of the EPA, William Ruckelshaus. He had just finished his speech, and I was going over some notes I had taken. Others were questioning some of his statements, and I had none. I had bought everything the man had said without challenge not so much because of the message but because of his title. The following column I wrote reflected just how naïve I was at the time. Later, I learned to question everything being said regardless of a person's status. Every big-time politician seems to have a pitch and a motive behind it.

29

Outdoors with Forda Birds

Ruckleshaus speaks the truth, I think.

Some 800 outdoor writers, families, and guests converged on Pensacola to open the 44th Annual Conference of the Outdoor Writers of America (OWAA). During the week of the conference, writers have a chance to listen, and, if the occasion calls for it, nail some of the leaders in industry and government to the proverbial wall during the many planned press conferences.

Some of the leaders who braved the onslaught of some of the top writers in the country were William D. Ruckelshaus, Administrator of Nixon's New Environmental Protection Agency; William E. Towell, Executive Vice President of the American Forestry Association; General Maxwell Evans Rich, Executive Vice President of the National Rifle Association; and many others.

Those absent were the Lieutenant Governor of the State of Florida who was being treated at an Ohio hospital for a virus and, most of all, the Governor of the State of Florida who evidently didn't care to knock heads with the group that had been a thorn in his side for a long time in reference to the now "kaput" Florida Barge Canal.

The most enlightening press conference was given by Mr. Ruckelshaus who, point by point, defined his job, personal position, and proposed action concerning many of the problems plaguing the environment of our country. For just about the first time, I heard a high government official talk in a language that is rather rare in politics—the truth.

That may seem a bit harsh, but it always seems that politicians that hang around for years and years have not feathered their party nest by telling the truth. Half truths and ambiguities seem to be the line of the day and in some cases falsehoods seem to be popular. Ruckelshaus made it quite clear that his job was to curb the senseless pollution of our environment and that in the six months of the Agency's short life changes are already beginning to take place. This nation has turned the environmental corner, according to Ruckelshaus, and it is my job as a writer and your job as citizens to see that these changes continue to take place.

Mr. Towell at the same press conference, called for writers and citizens alike to be moderate and let the agencies do their job. "They (writers and citizens) must take a responsible position of moderation based upon the evidence at hand and a full knowledge of the situation," stated Mr. Towell.

Questions that were brought up seemed to stem around the fact that the little guy (that's us) should base our judgment around much of the predigested information that seems to find its way from industrial public relations offices to the man on the street. How in the world are we as citizens going to find the truth if these agencies spend millions of dollars trying to hide it? How in the world can we as citizens be moderate in our actions when common sense tells us that we have to make a lot of noise to be heard over the programmed propaganda machines that each industry and governmental agency possesses?

This is one of the values of the conference. New writers, as well as the experienced, have the opportunity to learn and visualize the bigotry, hypocrisy, and bureaucracy that abound in our powerhouse industrial and governmental structures. In writing this column, I have seen the same in some of our state governmental agencies. Our environment is in trouble, and I intend to do my part to see that it is stabilized and improved. Some of the comments that I've received when I've taken a stand on an issue, such as the waterfowl refuge expansion, seem to state that Forda Birds, John Andreoni, is being a bit radical, is an alarmist, and is over-reaching. Well, my dear people, how do you want it? Do you want me to write the truth as I see it, which in turn gives you the opportunity to jump all over my back and prove me wrong, or do you want to read a bunch of half truths that we have been conditioned to accept as the truth.

I intend to speak out on issues in the future and when this column ever leaves the pages of the *Leader*, I hope no one will ever be able to say about Forda Birds what was once said about president Chester Arthur--"He has done well by not doing anything bad."

I will make mistakes in the future in this column. It's your responsibility to see that these mistakes are brought to my attention. Our country has environmental problems as well as many others. Just who is going to solve them if we, the people, don't?

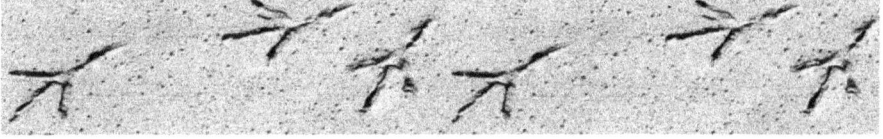

August 28, 1971

"I shear taxpayers, not sheep."

2009 finds Ohio in the middle of a budget crisis. Across the board cuts have been the rule rather than the exception in an attempt to create a balanced budget. Since the Ohio Division of Parks is funded by the general fund and not by dedicated money, it took more hits adding to the many it has already absorbed. The current economy is in turmoil and many states, including Ohio, are having a difficult time trying to come up with a balanced budget. California even planned to pay its bills with I.O.U.s.

Ohio's financial situation was no better in 1971. John J. Gilligan was elected governor in 1970 after two-term governor Jim Rhodes became ineligible to run. Once sworn in, his first priority was an attempt to come up with a balanced budget. As part of the plan, he initiated his famous "austerity program." Everyone took a hit, and the ODNR was not spared. 1,202 Natural Resource employees got the axe which was almost half of state employees that were let go.

ODNR Director, Bill Nye, attempted to get monies restored to his department when he testified before the Senate Finance Committee that not only was our environment at risk, but parks would be closed along with camping areas, beaches, and other facilities. "Unless there is a redirection of priorities and a rethinking in our values, we will destroy our environment as we build our society. What is the point of such foolishness?" said Nye.

Along with many other predictions, the state parks were closed for a short period of time. Budget shortfalls were eventually solved with the creation of Ohio's graduated income tax. Some think this was the direct cause of Gilligan losing to Jim Rhodes in 1974. The park closings supposedly had some effect. Others blame it on the fact that Gilligan was never afraid to speak his mind, although sometimes his mouth got him in trouble. For example, it is said that while attending a sheep shearing event at the Ohio State Fair, he was asked if he wanted to try his hand at the task. His press secretary choked when Gilligan said, "I shear taxpayers, not sheep."

After his loss to Rhodes, Gilligan's high profile political career came to an end. He was projected to be Jimmy Carter's vice presidential candidate. That never happened.

Regardless, the following column from 1971 could probably be run today. All one would need would be to change a name or two.

Outdoors with Forda Birds

State Government Levels ODNR

I find it a bit difficult to comment on the recent decisions that have come from the State Capitol stemming from the Legislature's inability to solve Ohio's budget problems and the Governor's Austerity Program. You see, I, like many other people in this state, am not an economist, governmental expert, or skilled politician. About the only qualifications I have that give me the license to say anything about the mess Ohio seems to be in is that I'm a citizen, I love my country, respect the form of government that made it great, and have the utmost confidence in the elected officials that represent us. Yes, I have confidence in our state government, but when they dealt the blow that caused the Department of Natural Resources to become, for all practical purposes, a "frozen" agency incapable of fulfilling its present responsibilities much less its future responsibilities, a great deal of that confidence went right down the drain.

Back in early June, I received releases from Columbus right after the House Republicans put through a budget that had more cuts in it than a Christmas turkey and actually allocated the Department of Natural Resources $800,000 less than the minimum continuation budget had called for. This, of course, eliminated the money asked for to expand the Department's activities as well as the proposed Task Force on Environmental Protection.

Director William B. Nye, testifying before the Senate Finance Committee, urged them to restore the $9.5 million that the House had cut. He mentioned the need for environmental protection to prevent a, "capitulation to special interests who are the only beneficiaries of an absence of anti-pollution efforts." He also warned that if the cuts were allowed to stand, personnel would have to be laid off forcing the closing of some state parks, camping areas, beaches, and other facilities.

When I read these reports, my view was one of indifference because I was confident that the legislature, after finishing their annual juggling act, would enact some sort of legislation that would show at least basic good judgment. As Mr. Nye said in his testimony, "Unless there is a redirection of priorities and a rethinking in our values, we will destroy our environment as we build our society. What is the point of such foolishness?" I don't think that many people would question the truth in that statement, and I felt that a large majority of legislators would have to listen to this warning and pay service to it if they were honest with themselves.

But, for some reasons, known or unknown by most of us, the legislature has failed to enact a budget and come up with some sort of means to fund it. The Governor has initiated an austerity program, and 2,840 state employees have gotten the axe--1,202 from the Department of Natural Resources. How can the Department of Natural Resources, in my opinion one of the most important agencies in the state, do a job with such a personnel cut? Why is it that almost one-half of the total layoffs came in the Department of Natural Resources? Why is it that present programs are stopped and parks closed? Why is it that millions of Ohioans are denied access to the parks that they pay for? Why is it that our own Park staff has been cut from 50 to 5 (at last count)? How in the world can a state government, supposedly working in good faith serving the people, permit our State of Ohio to get so fouled up? I don't know the answers to these questions and I'd bet a bundle that there are millions of people in Ohio that can't answer them either.

How does one try to find out something about these problems? Simple—contact your congressmen or other informed person. The only problem with that approach is that you receive a biased, party view. Ask a Republican what the problem is and he'll probably tell you that the Governor is using his austerity program as a club to ram through his budget and that negative reaction from the people will get the legislature in gear. That sounds like a good reason to me, but, on the other hand, if you ask a Democrat what's going on, he's more than likely going to tell you that the House Republicans are causing all the trouble by stopping every minority move before it starts. That sounds good to me as well. With that information, putting two and two together, I get five and that's foolishness.

I hope the legislature is honestly working to decide on the method to be used in funding the state's budget and not counting votes and worrying about the next election. I hope that no Democrat or Republican is cutting the throat of the Department of Natural Resources in an attempt to keep environmental control at a minimum in order to keep the door open for political parlor games with industries and influential individuals.

Speaking as a layman in the ministry of politics, it seems to me that the legislature must find a way to fund a budget, decide how the money is to be allocated, and hopefully, in my opinion, arrive at the conclusion that the

Department of Natural Resources receive not only adequate funds to continue at their present rate, but additional funds to initiate and expand programs that will protect and restore our natural resources for the benefit of all. That's no small task.

There's an old Army adage that says, "It's better to lose a battle by making the wrong decision than to lose a battle by making no decision." If the legislature doesn't make a decision, we're in a lot of trouble.

I think many people will agree that action should have been taken long ago and that action has to be taken now to break the stalemate that has already caused our Department of Natural Resources to stand in a corner and literally watch their accomplishments wash away, as well as the future hopes to do an even greater service to the people they serve. Action must be taken to maintain the other programs as well—education, welfare, etc.—to serve the betterment of our people. Yes, I believe that there are still a number of people like me that abide by decisions made by the government because we rely on professional judgment and the tradition and spirit of the law.

Mistakes have been made and will be made in the future operations of this state, politicians will continue to count votes, and political parties will probably always stand divided. So, Governor Gilligan, members of the Legislature, and all others who are in Columbus working to make Ohio a better place to live; establish a set of values, a set of values that not only call for the betterment of the people, but the betterment of our environment. Establish these values, and then let us know how we are going to support them. Granted, you're going to lose votes no matter which way you turn, but can you imagine the setback our Ohio will suffer if you do nothing? The common man wants to give his support to the people he chose to represent him. He surely can't support something that doesn't seem to exist, and man by his nature is going to support something or somebody—sometime. Every elected official in Ohio is losing this support, not because of his individual actions, but because he is a part of the group that is doing nothing. Once lost, this support will be hard to regain, and if you lose this support by setting Ohio back rather than letting her go forward, you deserve to lose it.

December 24, 1971

Christmas Spirit

I don't have a clue what inspired this next column other than it was going to appear on Christmas Eve. First, it had little to do with the outdoors, and second, it was a piece of fiction. There was no doubt I was going outside the box, but I decided to give it a shot and see how the readers would take it.

It was fantasy, pure and simple, but I tried to recall those early days when I believed in Saint Nick. I found the story was fun to write, and for a few moments, I regained a bit of my childhood. At the end, I wished the account was real. Even today, I like to let my imagination roam from time to time. Life seems so much simpler when I do. From the response I got back then, others felt the same way.

So, let's just move on by repeating this famous quote and let it go at that. "Yes, Virginia, there is a Santa Claus."

Merry Christmas from Forda Birds

Arf Bittlecow's Christmas Story

The sun was just starting to think about going down as I turned into the dry creek bed and headed up the old lane that led to Arf Bittlecow's place. Smoke swirled around the stone chimney and a soft glow radiated from the living room window as I stepped on the front porch and knocked on the front door.

"Merry Christmas, Arf!" I said.

36

"Well I'll be. Merry Christmas, Birds! Come on in and close the door."

As I walked into the living room, I was met by the warmth of a roaring fire in the cut-stone fireplace and greeted to a friendly yawn from Arf's old hound, Ball-a-fire, who was stretched the full length of the hearth rug. I took a seat next to Arf in front of the fire and gazed at a poster of Rosalie Adele Nelson, the original Lucky Strike Girl, as the flames sent ripples of light above the mantle and across her pretty but somewhat faded face. We just sat there, Arf and me, not saying a word, which was not uncommon in the Bittlecow house. Finally I turned to the old man and said, "What you been doing lately?"

Arf turned his head and showing me two eyes that looked like deep gashes cut in a ripe tomato, a nose the color of a half boiled lobster, and an Adam's apple that stuck out like an elbow on a gas pipe, said, "I've been fixin' a little present for Sandy Claus."

"What are you talking about, Arf?"

"Every year I brew up a special batch of apple brandy for Sandy when he stops by on Christmas Eve. It gets cold ridden that sled all over the place and when Sandy gets cold, a snort of that juice will pucker him up like fried potaters."

"You got to be kidding, Arf. You mean you still believe in Santa Claus at your age?"

"What's age got to do with it? All I know is that Sandy sets his sled down behind the barn every Christmas Eve to rest a spell and I got a jug out there for to warm him up. Last year he even wrote me a note." He dug in his pocket and pulled out a bedraggled piece of paper.

Dear Arf,

Thanks for the refreshment. One sip is enough to last me all night. That brandy is strong enough to tan a man's insides so he can swallow a live six-footed crab feet first. Arf, that stuffs strong enough to raise a blood blister on an old boot.

Thanks,
Your friend,
S. Claus

There was no doubt in my mind that Arf was serious, but any man who was testing a drink that made him think he swallowed a gas lamp was bound to believe anything. I had to find out more. "Arf," I said, "How long you been setting out presents for Santa?"

"Bout 16 years, I reckon. Yep, 16 years. Oh, I used to set out goodies when I was a little fella, but that don't count cause I quit."

"Why did you start again?"

The old man looked passed me, loaded his old clay pipe, and finally said, "Birds, what I'm going to tell you I ain't never told nobody else. People hear this story, they'd send me off to the funny farm for sure." He sat back in his rocker, reached down and scratched Ball-a-fire's ear, and began. "Well, it was December of 19 and 54. I had a old dog named Duke. Yep, me and Duke was closer than two flies on a cow chip. He used to sleep right there where Ball-a-fire's stretched out." Arf drew deeply on his ancient pipe and continued. "One night, Duke and me went to sleep in front of the fire. I woke up, but Duke—well, Duke didn't. I had to break ground with a pick, and I buried him by the grape vine out back."

Arf slowly got up, walked to the fire place, and placed another log on the fire. Then he turned and continued speaking in a much softer voice. "It was about this time of the evening, that Christmas Eve, maybe a little later, when I first noticed something strange going on outside. All the stock in the barn was makin noise and even the rooster crowed a couple of times. I grabbed my double-barrel and walked outside and then clear around the barn but I didn't see nothing. I remember there was snow on the ground and I didn't see any tracks, so I came back in the house and went to bed. Well, Birds, I don't know how long it was, but all of a sudden I heard the darndest commotion outside. I grabbed my shotgun and headed for the barn, bare feet and all. When I got there, everything quieted down. That barn was a sight to see. There was fresh bedding in the stalls, all the animals were feeding on fresh grain, and the cats were licking the sides of a large bowl of cream. All at once, I heard a gust of wind that rattled the slats on the barn, and then bells, and then a booming voice shouting, 'Merry Christmas, Arf Bittlecow!' I ran out the back of the barn and saw nothing but one big mess of tracks that all but covered the ground, There was weasel, rabbit, coon, fox, deer—all kinds of tracks and they headed off in all directions. Then I noticed a set of man tracks and they headed toward the house. I pulled back both hammers on my double and headed for the porch, looked around, but there wasn't nobody there. Then, when I was standin there like a gnat on a sugar spoon, I heard a noise, looked down, and saw a basket covered with rags. In them rags was a little hound pup. Looked just like Duke when he was a youngster. That's him down there on the floor, Birds."

Arf walked back to his chair and sat down. Then he turned and said, "The next Christmas Eve, I set out a pint of apple brandy behind the barn. I've done it every year since then and it's always gone when I check in the morning." Arf got up from his chair and started walking to the door. I knew it was time to leave. I looked at the old man and said, "Thanks for the story, Arf."

"Well, Birds, thanks for coming. You'd better hurry. It's getting late and Sandy don't cotton to a lot of strangers roamin around on Christmas Eve."

I started to drive down the lane and when I turned into the creek bed, I stopped the car, rolled down the window, and listened. Far off in the distance I swear I heard sleigh bells. Yes, it was sleigh bells alright, coming closer to Arf's place and that pint of apple brandy.

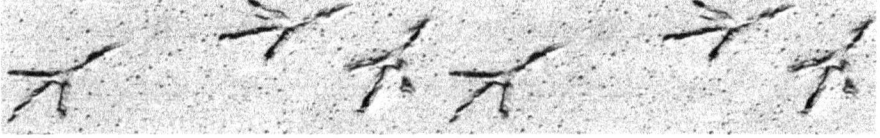

January 8, 1972

The Crystal Ball Worked

I don't specifically remember writing the following column, but I have a pretty good idea it was a desperation piece. In early January, there wasn't much going on outdoors, so I needed any generic idea that would give me enough required copy. For whatever reason, turkeys came to mind. I read somewhere that Benjamin Franklin had pushed for the turkey to be our national bird, which I found interesting. I had taken part in a failed turkey stocking attempt at Ft. Riley, Kansas in the 1960s, so that tied in. The only drawback was that there weren't more than a handful of turkeys in Ohio, so no one really cared.

While I was in Kansas, neighboring states were having some success with building a viable turkey population. I worked with some good wildlife management people at Kansas State University who knew that it was possible to restore a turkey population if pieces to the puzzle all fell into place. The turkey was an adaptable bird. Unfortunately, our stocking was doomed to fail. First, we released pen-raised birds. Second, they were the wrong strain. Ultimately, we did nothing more than release domesticated turkeys and hoped they could fend for themselves. They didn't.

From what I learned about turkeys at Ft. Riley, I was convinced that game management people could and would bring back turkeys to Ohio someday. I went so far as to say that Auglaize County might have a few birds running around, although I had a rough time believing it.

The rest is history. In the early fall of 2008, Ohio had an estimated flock of 200,000 turkeys, and hunters harvested more than 20,000 during the 2009 spring hunting season. Auglaize County has a flock estimated between 600 and 1000, and the local bag was almost 50 birds. As far as Kansas is concerned, stockings in the early 1970s took off, and today there are Rio Grande, Eastern, and crossbreeds all over the state. I believe with appropriate permits, Kansas hunters can take six birds total during the spring and fall seasons.

Since the Ohio turkey is one of the state's greatest game management success stories, I thought it significant to include what I had to say about this great game bird almost 40 years ago.

Outdoors with Forda Birds

Let's Talk About Turkeys

A long time ago when our ancestors were trying to select a bird for our national emblem, Ben Franklin casually peered over his bifocals and suggested the wild turkey. As far as he was concerned, there was no doubt in his mind which bird should represent our country. Besides that, the bald eagle was on the old philosopher's black-list.

In 1784 Franklin wrote, "I wish the Bald Eagle had not been chosen as the Representative of our country; like those among Men who live by Sharping and Robbing, he is generally poor, and often very lousy. The Turkey is a much more respectable bird, and withal a true original Native of America."

Yes, a turkey may have been a more logical choice than the bald eagle. Turkeys are restricted almost entirely to North America while the bald eagle has a world wide reputation. Turkeys were used by the Indians and domesticated by the Aztecs in Mexico long before Columbus arrived. The colonists harvested the wild birds at will and all settlers made good use of the turkey as an important source of food. It isn't difficult to see why Franklin made his choice.

But, as the population increased and forests fell to agriculture, the native turkey population declined steadily. We still, however, had a nation of turkey eaters, but their dinner table was filled by a domesticated bird that was bred for taste and bulk.

A few years ago, the chances of survival for the turkey were slim. However, management and restoration programs have brought the turkey back in sizeable numbers with many states having a hunting season in various degrees. Even Ohio has a limited turkey season in certain counties with the hunter quota being filled by permits. The southern states have the larger populations of these game birds, but the Rio Grande subspecies has flourished in the western states.

Probably one of the greatest success stories in turkey propagation comes from Nebraska. Stocking in the north and western parts of this state have led to phenomenal results. One of the prime areas is the Pine Ridge Country, where the Black Hills spill over from South Dakota into part of Nebraska.

Kansas had a very small turkey population along the Oklahoma border, but wild trapping and transplants from the far southwestern edge of the state in the northeastern edge may develop a stable population. The main reason I mentioned Kansas is that at one time I was the Wildlife Conservation Officer at Ft. Riley.

It was there that I learned the hard way about the problems that come up when improper stocking takes place. I was asked by the powers-to-be to investigate the possibilities of stocking turkeys on the post. After talking with Kansas State University professors and the wildlife people at Pratt, I prepared a rather lengthy report that stated in brief that it was highly improbable that this program would work. My report was ignored by a certain general who said, "My program will work because I said it will work!" The next day I was on my way to a large game farm near Abilene to pick up 100 pen raised Merriam turkeys that they just happened to have left over at a special price ($7.00 each). It was a gala affair as the high brass, myself, my prison labor, and a crew of photographers headed for the wide open spaces of Ft. Riley. Pictures were taken of each officer holding a turkey and then the birds were released. I have a file of these pictures but according to a statement printed on the back I'm not permitted to use them for some reason or the other. However, if anyone wants to see an 8X10 glossy of a general loving up a 15 pound turkey, I might be able to arrange it.

Needless to say, when I left to go over seas, our program had turned out to be a disastrous flop. Oh, some roosted alright. They set up house keeping in a steam engine that was being displayed on the main highway going through the post. They took over the 4th, 5th, and 6th hole of the officer's golf course. They destroyed all of the officers' wives' gardens, even the general's wife was not spared as her garden was one of the first to go. They invaded barnyards, backyards and stockyards. Five of these "wild" birds were even spotted walking down the main street of Manhattan, Kansas some 20 miles away from where they were released. These were pen raised birds and studies and my report told exactly what would happen to them.

Another example of poor planning took place on the eastern edge of Kansas on the Missouri border. After WWII, Missouri started a project to restore their wild turkey population. By 1960, there was a limited season for residents. Kansas decided to increase their population of turkeys by releasing pen raised birds along her border. The results almost caused a war between the two states. Instead of the pen raised birds turning wild as they mixed with the present flocks, they tamed the wild birds and in the process caused the state of Missouri to lose quite a bit of the population of turkeys they had worked so hard to build up.

41

From these mistakes they learned, and today the population of turkeys is increasing in these two states. The golden rule that Kansas and Missouri now follow is that only birds trapped in the wild and relocated will survive and flourish. Nebraska, parts of Colorado, and the Dakotas have also found this to be true.

Yes, turkeys can be managed and restored to a stable population as long as they have their brushy cover, water, grain, seeds, acorns, beechnuts, wild grapes, and other fruit. Who knows, maybe some day the turkey will again populate all of the areas that it did when our ancestors first stepped off the boat. It might be possible to have a few turkeys running around Auglaize county one of these years. Regardless, turkeys are the kings of North American upland game birds and have the right to flourish. Even though the bald eagle is one of the most beautiful birds we have, Ben Franklin did have a point, didn't he?

January 15, 1972

Berlet Breaks Guinness Shooting Record

This area has always been considered trapshooting country and in the process has produced some premier competitors. If you mention the sport anywhere in Ohio or in the nation, for that matter, Dave Berlet is a name that is known by everyone, and why shouldn't it be. He's been involved in the sport since he was a baby when he attended his first Grand American in the arms of his parents. Through 2008, he has attended the last 65 and competed in 52 of them.

What trap honors has Berlet received over his 52 years of competition? The list is long. He was named Clay Target Champion of America at the 2000 Grand. He was four-time High Ohio 16 yard average leader. In numerous years, he was on the All-American Team. He was inducted into the Ohio Trapshooting Hall of Fame in 1995. No, he never won the Grand American, but was runner-up in 1961, and the list goes on and on.

The most unique recognition Berlet ever received, at least in my eyes, was establishing a new shooting record for the *Guinness Book of World Records*. The challenge was breaking the most clay targets in an hour. Ultimately, Berlet was chosen by Remington to challenge the record, and after training for the event, proceeded to tear the old one apart. In 60 minutes, he managed to break an astonishing 1,572 clay birds. According to my math, counting the birds dropped, he was shooting at a target every other second.

I've known Berlet for many years, and I consider him a friend. He's easy going, and is considered by most to be one of the "good ole boys." The flip side is that whenever he competes, regardless of the competition, he intends to win. Those of us who have watched Berlet in his competitive mode know that if you cross the line and distract him, he won't be a happy camper. Even more, if you happen to be the guilty party that gets him irritated, be prepared to pay a price.

Regardless, Dave Berlet is a legitimate trapshooting legend, and because of that, the column I wrote about his Guinness record back in 1972 earned a place in this volume.

Outdoors with Forda Birds

Guinness Record Blasted

Dave Berlet, who last September set a new worlds record by breaking 1,572 clay targets in 60 minutes, is featured in the January-February issue of *Dupont Magazine*. According to the article and my *Guinness Book of World Records*, the previous record was held by Joseph Wheater of Kingstonupon-Hull, Yorkshire, England. Mr. Wheater, at Bedford on September 21, 1957, broke 1308 targets in one hour. He shot 1000 targets in 42 minutes 22.5 seconds.

Dave is known as one of the best, if not the best trap shooter in the area, and when I got wind of his attempt and eventual breaking of the existing record, I wasn't the least bit surprised. Now, after reading the article in *Dupont Magazine*, looking at the second hand of my watch, and trying to hold a shot gun to my shoulder until it began to get mighty heavy, Dave's record has to be one of the most astounding feats in shooting history. Here are the statistics as quoted in the article:

> 18 minutes 40 seconds—472 hits out of 500 targets thrown;
> 28 minutes 52 seconds—713 hits out of 750 targets thrown;
> In the next 68 seconds, Berlet broke an additional 31 targets;
> 30 minutes, the halfway mark—743 hits in 781 tries;
> 38 minutes 30 seconds—1000 targets hit (a new world record);
> 60 minutes—1,572 hits out of 1,659 targets thrown.

A new world record breaking the old one by 262 targets.

The number of targets fired at and the percentage hit is not that impressive to good trap shooters, and Berlet, who recorded the first 200 straight at the 1964 Grand American and had the third highest 16 yard average in the nation for 1967, will agree. These good shooters shoot thousands of targets each year. The element that makes this record so amazing is that it all transpired in 60 short minutes. His record breaking feat was equivalent approximately to shooting at a target every two seconds for an hour and breaking more than 95 percent.

Dave told me that all he did in preparation for the event was to hold a shotgun with a weight fastened on the end of the barrel to build up his endurance. I'm sure this was a great help, but he failed to mention the fact that he possesses the intense concentration that makes the good athlete the best in his field.

Will Berlet consider trying to break his own record? He doesn't think so, and I hope he never does. I can't afford spending $6 for another revised, deluxe edition of the *Guinness Book of World Records*.

JANUARY 24 DEADLINE FOR ORDERING TREES

This is just a reminder that anyone planning to order trees through the Auglaize Chapter of the Izaak Walton League must have their order and check in to the organization by their January 24 meeting. Orders should be sent to the Auglaize Chapter, Izaak Walton League, PO Box 208, St. Marys, Ohio. Individuals or groups that purchase trees are under no obligation to the organization or any of its members.

I was planning to do a little fishing at the "hot water" in Celina, but after talking to my friend at the First National Bank, I don't think I will. Last Friday the crappies were hitting extremely well with some 12 to 14 inches being reported. But, as usual, I was a day late and a dollar short. When I arrived there last Saturday morning, the water was not being pumped into the area and ice was starting to form. Needless to say, the fishing was at a standstill.

I just called the fellow at the First National again to see if it's warming up. He really must have a boring job. He isn't much of a conversationalist either. Maybe I hurt his feelings. Let's see. I dialed 4-2366, said "Hello, how ya doing." He said something about an auto loan. "How's everything going?" He said, "Time 6:17, Temperature 9 Below." Then I asked him if it was going to warm up and he hung up on me. Gee, I wonder what I said wrong.

Editors note: As a public service, the bank installed an automated call-in system that provided time and temperature. This, of course, was before the automated signs we see at most banks today. That's right, St. Marys phone numbers were five digits.

March 25, 1972

An Engineering Marvel

I grew up along the Miami-Erie Canal. I lived above the family confectionery store that nestled safely between three bars and a barber shop. Today, my old backyard is a parking lot, but when I was young, it was a recreational spot used by just about every kid from the east end of town. On occasion, some west-enders ventured onto our grounds, but it didn't happen very often.

As I got older, I expanded my turf and knew just about every square inch of canal from the bulkhead on the East Bank of Lake St. Marys, down the feeder, then north to the 40 Acre Pond and beyond. It provided many great places to hunt and fish. As a kid, I really had it made. I was a true canal rat.

A number of years later, I was teaching at McBroom School. I recall one of our annual open houses where a few interested parents usually made an appearance. On this occasion, one wiry, feisty looking dad remained until everyone had moved on. I had made mention about being a towny and growing up on the canal. This fellow trumped all of my stories and told me things about the canal I never knew. His name was Jim Kite.

Jim always had a dream to put water back in the canal from Lake Loramie to Delphos. He was tireless in his efforts, but it never came to fruition. He did manage to ramrod a project to put water in a mile section of canal just north of Lock 8. A small concrete dam was constructed, the canal bottom was cleaned of all brush, briars, and brambles, and for a short period of time, we had water. We even canoed it one time.

I don't know how many service clubs we talked to over an 18th month period about the canal, but Jim was the star at all of them. His slide show was excellent and contained pictures of such unique items as the half-way concrete marker. I still remember seeing T122/C122, the distances to Toledo and Cincinnati, carved in the monument.

Jim Kite always referred to himself as a lake rat, but he was a true canal rat as well. I wonder if his slide show still exists? Regardless, it was Kite's influence that made me look at the Miami-Erie Canal as an engineering marvel, as something special. Finally, he was a good man.

Miami & Erie Canal: The Eighth Wonder of the World?

It seems the more I find out about the Miami & Erie Canal, the less I really know about it. That statement might sound a bit off base, but the fact remains that for each question I get answered about this engineering marvel, I wind up with five new ones that I can't answer. It's these questions that I can't answer but only guess at that lead me to believe that the Miami & Erie Canal is one of man's greatest physical accomplishments.

Like the "ten best dressed" award, history has what is known as the "Seven Ancient Wonders of the World." From the Pyramids of Egypt to the Mausoleum at Halicarnassus, the criteria that the historians used to give this title appeared to be size, length of time to construct, number of men used, and the difficulty of the project. For example, history tells us that the Great Pyramid of Khufu took 20 years to build, contained 2,300,000 stones weighing 2 ½ tons each, and had a labor force of 100,000 unwilling workers.

Let's apply these guide lines to the Miami & Erie and with a bit of "guesstimation" see what we come up with. First of all, it took 22 years to complete this project. The completed canal was 244 miles long and contained 105 locks. Much of the land was still virgin timber and had to be cleared before digging could begin. Trees were cut with axes and stumps were removed without the use of blasting powder. If any of you have ever tried to remove a stump, you'll appreciate the historical account that tells of trees 7 feet in diameter being felled by axe, and a crew of 7 men and 2 horses removing 20 to 40 stumps a day.

Unlike ancient times when Pharaohs, Caesars, and kings forced their subjects to build these ancient monuments, the canals were built by willing people at the demand of the people themselves. How many men worked on the project during those 22 years? I can't answer the question, but records show that 1700 worked on the east and west banks of Lake St. Marys, 500 men worked on the stretch between Loramie and St. Marys, and contracts were let on sections ranging from 1 to 5 miles. From these figures it might be safe to say that hundreds of thousands worked on the canal during its construction.

Another interesting question that is probably impossible to answer deals with the loss of life during the construction. History never seems to record the personal side of the story, and only bits and pieces of information can be found. More information might be hidden somewhere in old records, but I have yet to see a mortality list. Most of the workers on the canals were German and Irish immigrants. When they got off the boat, they were met by men who offered them high wages for their strong backs. These immigrants traveled by canal to what is now the western side of Ohio and began to earn their keep.

These workers arrived in this area and were greeted by swampland and forests that kept the sun from view. They not only faced the hard labor, but were constantly fearful of disease. From time to time cholera would strike, but malaria was ever present. The workers felt that alcohol would protect them and one report shows that 45 barrels of whiskey were consumed to every 42 barrels of flour. Workers were naturally fearful of malaria and since the labor force had to be kept up, wages were stated in terms of money and whiskey. Top pay during these tunes was $3 a day and 16 jiggers of whiskey.

How many men died during these times? Only an occasional comment can be found. It was said in one account that in crossing malaria infested areas, a man died for every 6 feet of finished canal. According to my calculations that would mean that between here and Toledo, all of which was malaria country, approximately 100,000 men lost their lives. That appears to be an outlandish figure, but history also tells us that standard procedure called for cemeteries along the canal to be closed when the dead numbered 1000. The question then comes up as to where those cemeteries are located. I've never heard of one, yet I wonder if they may not have been marked. Were the immigrants that came into this area carried on records somewhere? If not, how will we ever know? I was also told that there is a picture in one of the county historical societies north of here that shows human skulls on fence posts. This picture was taken, supposedly, at the turn of the century and the skulls were found in the washed out canal bank. Were people so impersonal that they buried their dead right on the spot as they worked? It doesn't seem likely, but if it were true, you can be sure that this type of action would not find its way in a history book.

I, surely, am not a canal historian and don't claim to be. But the fact is that the 244 miles of the Miami & Erie Canal, as well as the other 700 plus miles of canals in this state, make up an accomplishment of man that is beyond imagination. Wouldn't this make the canal another "Wonder of the World?"

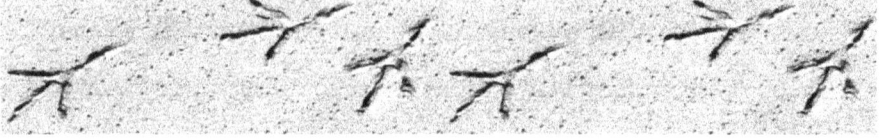

May 13, 1972

The First National Hunting & Fishing Day

Over a century ago, hunters and fishermen were the earliest and strongest supporters of conservation and wildlife management. As the U.S. continued its rapid growth and development, these sportsmen recognized that many species of fish and game were being threatened by the unregulated uses of these resources. President Teddy Roosevelt, an avid sportsman, called for the first laws restricting the commercial slaughter of the nation's wildlife. These new rules affected market hunters, including the ones in our area who killed and sold millions of ducks and geese that migrated through here both in the fall and spring. The same applied to commercial fishermen who shipped countless barrels of fish taken from Lake St. Marys to market.

These pioneer conservation activists called for scientific game management, fishing, hunting, and trapping licenses, and taxes on sporting equipment to fund state conservation agencies. As a result, the wildlife development protocol we follow now has brought about some of the most dramatic fish and wildlife success stories across the country. In Ohio, these successes are more than evident with the walleye fishery in Lake Erie and our huge resident flock of Canada geese. Turkey, a species once considered extinct in Ohio, is hunted in all 88 counties and numbers in the thousands. White-tailed deer, a rare species in Ohio less than 60 years ago, are now the number one game animal hunted in the state.

As this conservation movement grew, more and more individuals took up the banner. Along with the money they generated, sportsmen worked countless hours to protect and improve millions of acres of vital habitat. They formed many organizations active today that focus on maintaining and fostering a viable environment for countless species, not just those considered targets of the rod and gun.

In the 1960s, sportsmen became discouraged when many people showed an ignorance of the role hunters and fishermen play in the conservation movement. This was especially so as anti hunting and fishing groups came out of the woodwork, became more vocal, and started to grow. As a result of these feelings, National Hunting and Fishing Day was born. No doubt, this was a significant moment in time.

Outdoors with Forda Birds

NHF Day

On September 23, 1972, millions of Americans will observe National Hunting and Fishing Day during which hunting and fishing groups in this country will hold open house and celebrate the tremendous contribution of sportsmen to conservation and the intelligent management of natural resources.

NHF Day got its start when Senator Thomas J. McIntyre introduced S. J. Resolution 117 in Congress last year. He called upon President Nixon to declare the fourth Saturday of each September "National Hunting and Fishing Day."

Response was quick as 33 senators immediately co-sponsored the resolution. Representative Bob Sikes offered H. J. Resolution 798 in the House. Hundreds of prominent legislators in the states, governors, mayors, and other leaders offered their cooperation.

What takes place on this day? First of all it is a day set to recognize the sportsman for the job he's done over the years in support of the environment, fish, animals, and other resources by his time, money, and labor.

Secondly, it is a day on which countless outdoor groups of various types will tell not only the more than 55 million hunters and fishermen in this country the importance of the sportsman, but all who will listen. Through open house displays, exhibits, films, and craft demonstrations, together with participation in sport, the American people will be given an object lesson in protection of the environment and clean sport which builds character while it insures healthy skills and guarantees a steady population of fish and game for years to come.

I assume that some who read this column will think it terrible that a day be set side to condone the senseless slaughter of millions of animals, game birds, and fish, but that can be expected. Even though I don't agree with that philosophy, I do respect it. On the other hand, I have no respect for the alarmist who stands up and screams at the sportsman while at the same time, he watches the countryside being polluted, dredged, drained, and paved.

This group of anti-hunting and fishing "nuts" is stronger than most people think. The Washington D.C. based Committee for Humane Legislation lists a total ban on hunting as one of its five goals for the 92nd Congress. "Friends of Animals" from New York City sponsors expensive full-page newspaper ads that urge readers to "stop the murder of wildlife" by writing President Nixon. I just wonder if these groups realize that taking away the $235 million dollars that sportsmen pay to support wildlife just might cause an even bigger slaughter.

Doing away with hunting and fishing is a dangerous idea and the movement is being headed by even more dangerous people. Here is an example of some of the comments being made by the extreme anti-hunting and fishing crusader. The following was heard on a New York radio station. "The only good time I have during the entire hunting season is at the end of the season when they say 27 hunters were killed. It's my fondest wish that all these people are terrible shots and they'll all be dead at the end of the hunt." If this is an example of the leadership of the anti-hunting fishing movement, I'm scared.

The fact of the matter is, however, that National Hunting and Fishing Day does exist and with the support of governmental leaders and organizations such as the National Wildlife Federation, OWAA, Boy Scouts of America, National Rifle Association, Izaak Walton League, and others, it will be a success.

We have a number of good outdoor organizations in our area. It seems to me that it would be beneficial to area people if these groups planned some sort of program for NHF Day this fall. It might also be appropriate for our local leaders to add their support to this day and give some credit to the sportsmen of this area for the help they're giving in assuring that wildlife will be around for a long time to come.

May 27, 1972

Wallace Shooting Sparks Gun Legislation Debate

On May 15, 1972, 22 year-old Art Bremer plunged through a crowd who had just finished hearing Alabama Governor George Wallace give a presidential campaign speech. He emptied his .38 caliber revolver hitting Wallace numerous times. One of the bullets permanently paralyzed the governor from the waist down.

As a result of this senseless shooting, the cry for stricter gun legislation began to swell in Washington, and the debate was on...again. In less than ten years, America had a president assassinated, then the president's brother as he ran for the highest office in the land. Shooting politicians seemed to be a good means of communication. Unfortunately, the message was usually convoluted, and the shooters weren't playing with a full deck.

In the case of Bremer, history shows he really wanted to shoot Richard Nixon. Tight presidential security prevented this from happening, so his next choice of targets was Governor Wallace. Wallace, of course, was known at that time for his strong racial views. Evidently, Bremer wasn't concerned about that issue or any other that Wallace held. All he wanted to do was shoot someone famous and become famous.

As a result of the shooting and its aftermath, I felt the need to comment on the gun-control issue. Of course, I had my views and always believed that guns didn't kill people, people killed people. That was my mind set when I wrote the following column. However, in the spirit of being open minded, I agreed that cheap handguns, known as "Saturday Night Specials," be eliminated. I also suggested that any crime involving the use of a gun should carry an additional, severe penalty. It made sense to me.

I didn't receive many local comments from the column, but I did find out later that a national pro-gun organization received it from a clipping service and labeled me as a gun opponent because I slammed cheap handguns. I carried that handle for a year or two. So, you read the column and see if you

52

can figure out my views on gun control. I thought they were pretty obvious.

Outdoors with Forda Birds

Gun Legislation is a Wasted Effort

Ever see the cartoon where the mouse approaches the sleeping cat and then with much bravado taunts and teases the unknowing feline to the amusement of the other mice? Then the cat wakes up and the story changes. This is the situation that the movement for stronger gun legislation is in today.

A few weeks ago, a writer could have made any comment he wished about gun legislation and probably would have been at least tolerated by all. Today, shortly after the senseless act that sent George Wallace to the hospital paralyzed from the waist down, any writer who speaks out against gun legislation is just like a mouse approaching the cat when it's awake. The writer is going to draw criticism from well meaning but misguided individuals who think or suggest that additional gun laws are a cure-all for assassinations and crime. It's the opinion of this writer that this, "ain't necessarily so."

I'm not against gun legislation in principle because it's to the benefit of the gun owner to have a record of ownership on file somewhere. What I am against is that if licensing of all weapons, for example, comes into play, the bureaucratic structure that comes with it will add one more batch of administrivia, paperwork, forms, etc. that the gun owner must support. The innocent foots the bill, while the criminal, by nature, is exempt.

Comments have been made that most of the killings in the United States are of the explosive variety, no pun intended. In a moment of anger or frustration, wives have been known to shoot their husbands and husbands their wives. Fathers shoot sons and sons shoot fathers. Mothers shoot daughters and so on. Gun legislation as proposed will have little effect on these killings. If a gun isn't handy and a person is in a mental state that would cause him to commit murder, I'm confident that the murder would be accomplished. To me this theory would call for knife legislation, registering of all heavy objects such as ball bats, wrenches, bricks and anything else weighing over two pounds.

This is a poor time for anyone to even be thinking about additional gun legislation. Politicians across the country have a ready-made bandwagon to jump on, and I imagine that many of them will be singing loudly before the next election. No laws should be built on emotion and emotion does take a place in the discussion today. After the Kennedy assassinations, we had the development of the Federal Control Act of 1968. In short, this legislation was sound, but the fact is this legislation was designed without the majority in mind. It may accomplish what it was intended to accomplish, but regardless, the person who wants a gun to shoot someone can obtain one no matter what the law says. The man charged with shooting Governor Wallace was in violation of local and state firearms control laws before he even fired that gun, He lived in Detroit, a city that has a terrific murder rate yet has extremely strong city ordinances against handguns.

What's the answer? It appears to me that the following two measures would solve many more problems than any additional gun legislation aimed at the sportsman. The "Saturday Night Special" bill introduced last year by Senator Birch Bayh which would prohibit the sale or delivery of crudely made and unsafe handguns not suited for sporting purposes should be adopted. Secondly, criminals using firearms during their activities should receive automatic and severe punishment. For example, legislation introduced by Rep. Bob Casey (D-Texas) calls for a sentence of not less than 10 years for the first offense and 25 years for the second offense and subsequent offenses.

In this day and age, it appears that our laws are being relaxed and our police forces are being held back to assure the criminal of his rights. It appears that our high courts go to extremes to bring about "justice". Recent decisions concerning integration, pornography, criminal rights, etc. lead me to believe that the plurality isn't being considered. A criminal has rights like everyone else. Hogwash! To me, a criminal loses his rights as soon as he commits an act against the society. Gun legislation aimed against the non-sporting weapons may have some benefit. Making it expensive for the criminal to use firearms in his "trade" in terms of years in prison would have more. Would you believe that sportsmen are citizens too? And, being citizens bound by the laws and sanctions of the society in which we live, we also have rights, one of which is the constitutional right to keep and bear arms for lawful use.

July 15, 1972

Recycling is a Mindset

I'm not sure when I started to recycle. I know I've been doing it in some fashion for more than 60 years. I grew up during WWII, and anyone who made that trip can recall some of the strange things people started to do. I learned about black-outs and ration stamps, helped my mother make homemade margarine, pulled weeds in the Victory Garden, and saved any form of metal we used, including silver gum wrappers.

Of course, my first real recycling experience had nothing to do with saving the planet. I was probably in grade school when the need for spending money had our small band of brothers going door to door gathering newspapers and any other saleable junk. We loaded it on a homemade four-wheel cart and drug the load to the local junkyard where we received what we thought was a fair price. After a couple of trips, all of us could afford to spend a nickel for a coke, and the rest of the cash was spent on fishing tackle or a new baseball.

I quickly outgrew the trips to the junkyard and never gave recycling another thought until I started writing this column. By then, words like environment, nonrenewable resource, and recycling were in my everyday vocabulary. However, I still didn't take recycling seriously because I wasn't about to have people seeing me haul paper, cans, and other metals to the local junk establishments. It was a pride thing, and quiet frankly, it wasn't worth the effort.

Then, the newly formed local chapter of the Izaak Walton started a program where people could take their paper, glass and metal to a central collection point and the rest is history. The League made a little money in the beginning and then gave other organizations the chance to share in the wealth and the work.

The rest is history. Lines of cars still go to the city garage to drop of their recyclables. It's a habit now. Before long, the city set up a system where people could put their papers, cans, and bottles in bins and set them out for pickup. Recycling has become a mindset, and that's a good thing. A lot of environmentally proactive people started recycling in the area. I just wrote about it on occasion.

Outdoors with Forda Birds

Project Recycle

Next Saturday, July 22, the Izaak Walton League will begin maintaining a collection point for glass, paper, metal, and rags to be recycled. This project is considered a public service and is being handled in conjunction with the Lima-Troy Area Community Action Program Council of the United Auto Workers and with the assistance of the City of St. Marys.

The article in last night's *Evening Leader* explained quite clearly what was to be collected and that plans were in the making of turning the project into a monthly happening. I don't imagine that the paper was off the press for more than five minutes when my phone rang and someone started making comments about the "Izaak Newton Paper Drive." With those words still ringing through my head as they went in one ear and out the other, I started to think if people knew exactly what recycling was all about.

I'm sure quite a few have a good idea what recycling is but for those who don't, it simply means that glass, metal, and rags are collected, processed and reused. This accomplishes two things—it keeps this junk from finding its way to a landfill or being burned, and it saves the natural resources it takes to replace it.

Recycling isn't new and St. Marys isn't the only place in the U.S.A. where a project such as this is being operated. We, as a people, are finally awakening to the critical need for recycling. All paper that is used by the State of Ohio is recycled, saving countless trees. Much of the paper, I believe, that is being used in our city has been processed and is being used again. Concerned people in this country have turned in billions of bottles and cans and industry has developed plants that take garbage straight from the truck and reprocess it to save resources. Salvage pays the processing costs.

Yes, the people in this country are starting to see that our resources are not limitless as we thought. The U.S. reuses 20 percent of the 60 million tons of paper produced annually. Research has shown a way to convert organic wastes and paper into a product resembling crude oil by using high pressure steam. Research also shows that ground up glass can replace gravel in asphalt highways and that ground-up rubber tires mixed with asphalt make a crack resistant road that lasts four times longer than conventional roads. The U.S. junks 7 million cars annually and the U.S. Steel production now contains 55 percent scrap.

Something must be done to save our resources and apathy is not the answer. Whether we like it or not, we are all members of the most wasteful nation the earth has ever seen. Each American throws out a ton of garbage and wastepaper every year. Landfill space is running out and the small communities like St. Marys don't want the big city garbage. Incinerators to burn it cannot keep pace with the refuse and in the process add to air pollution.

It's obvious that recycling is essential. It is also obvious that it is the responsibility of every man, woman, and child to do his or her part in eliminating waste that will eventually strangle us. It isn't a pretty picture and it's not a picture made by an alarmist. But, the fact remains that we are faced by a problem, and we had better be thinking how to solve it. Our part may be small, but wouldn't it be nice to give a helping hand to assure that our children will have a decent world to live in—life in harmony with nature? With a bit of effort, we can help make this hope a reality.

Take your glass, paper, rags and aluminum cans to the city garage, North Chestnut, next Saturday, 9 a.m. to 1 p.m., for recycling. Do your bit to help this project.

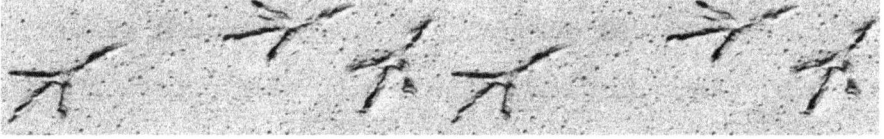

September 23, 1972

The Birth of K.C. Geiger Park

When I was a young kid, my outdoor world gravitated along the Miami-Erie Canal. Crossing South Street and heading south past the White Mountain Creamery took me to new and interesting stomping grounds. First was the train trestle where I liked to huddle against the wall and feel the rumble of gigantic steam engines as they passed by. The Boyer property was the next stop. There were some decent frogs to be had in the abandoned ponds that sat there. Then came the city dump. Of course, it had a smell all its own. There was always a fresh supply of rotting garbage and the rats loved it. The number of rat hunts that took place there will never be known.

Twenty years later, someone came up with the idea that the dump would make a great city park. I don't know who originated the idea, but Ed Stepleton came to me and asked if I'd help with a campaign to get the voters to support the idea with their dollars. The campaign theme was "Do You Care?" A park sounded like a good idea to me, and the rest is history.

We pulled every stunt in the book to get voter support. If I remember correctly, we had a sky diver land on the 50 yard line of the football stadium during a pre-game show streaming a "Do You Care Banner." I took it upon myself to elicit support from some big shots. I wrote Governor Gilligan and received a nice letter urging the voters to do their duty. He killed any impact he might have had when he referred to the proposed park sitting along the beautiful blue waters of the St. Marys River. A spokesman from Dick Nixon's office told me the President never stuck his nose in local city business. Regardless, it was a grand campaign and the voters turned the issue down.

So how did we eventually get the park? I think former City Service Director Kenny Hegemann had a great deal to do with it. I understand he found some extra capital improvement money that started the ball rolling. After that, some grant money made its way into the project. Most of all, there were countless volunteer man-hours that helped make the park what it is today.

Later named K.C. Geiger Park, the old city dump is now a parcel of ground that is enjoyed by everyone who goes there. I'd like to think that if a park improvement issue was put on the ballot again, St. Marys voters would approve it. The new theme would probably be, "Yes, We Care."

Here's the puff column I wrote promoting the park. I apologize for the part about respecting Gilligan and Nixon. I never really cared for Nixon.

Outdoors with Forda Birds

A City Recreational Area: Do You Care?

From time to time I try to analyze the readers of this column to see how they might react to what I've written. It's not unusual because all good writers do it, as well as the rest of us who are trying to be good. Depending on the column, I've come to the conclusion that many take these weekly offerings seriously, many are able to pick out the subtle comments I occasionally make, many enjoy the frequent attempts at humor, many take every work with tongue in cheek, many readers can take it or leave it, and many simply take it out with the garbage on Saturday night. What it all boils down to is that the readers of *The Evening Leader* and "Outdoors with Forda Birds" have opinions and contrasting points of view. The right to have opinions is the American way but it creates problems for a writer who is trying to reach as large an audience as possible. Because the ideas, thoughts, and views of people are so diversified, very seldom can the writer present material that hits everyone, but, once in awhile the opportunity arises. Yes, once in awhile an issue comes before his readership that affects every citizen of the community. And, being a citizen of the community and a voice exposed in the news media, he is obliged to take a stand. The issue I'm referring to is the City Recreational Issue that will appear on the November ballot.

When I was in Idaho a couple of summers ago, I had the fortune of meeting one of the top men in the newspaper business. During our conversation he made it perfectly clear that what you write is your opinion and yours alone. This doesn't mean that others don't share this opinion, but what it does mean is that your opinion was formulated by using personal judgment and logic. He also said that a writer has the responsibility to tell the truth to the best of his ability and as long as he does this he can never be condemned. Criticized, yes! Condemned, no! Now, to the issue.

The proposed recreational area on the property including the farm land of Weston Paper is something that demands the interest of every citizen of St. Marys. This is my home town and for the first time that I can remember, there appears to be a spark that could make our community grow and prosper. Thinking into the future and planning for the future bring about growth and without this idea, a small community such as ours becomes stagnant and eventually disappears. This city has always supported community development. Our schools are prime examples, the hospital is another. Our major industry, Goodyear, must look into the future and their growth and success depend on it.

Now, the citizens of St. Marys are being asked to look into the future and support an issue that will add to the list of credits that make this town one of the best in the country. To me, there is no other way to go but to support this issue. Like all other issues there is no absolute. One can find things wrong with it. But, weighing the good with the bad, the issue is sound and beneficial to the city.

One of the biggest complaints against the recreational area will be an increase in taxes. My answer to this is, Hogwash! I'm a tax payer too and additional taxes don't make me happy UNLESS they do some good for me or for my community. It takes money to pay for the services we all scream about and dollars spent to make my home town a better place to live are worth spending.

The other complaint will be the type of services offered. I, for example, would like to have a trap and skeet range located on the proposed site. I would also like to have a white water canoe course, and an Olympic ski jump. Others would like to have an Olympic indoor pool. All of these, it appears to me are beyond the cost capabilities of this town and its citizens at this time. The recreation area that is being planned will have areas for future expansion, but the basic concept, I believe, is to create an area that will service all ages without putting us in debt for the next 480 years.

Yes, there are bound to be negative opinions about this proposed park, but I for one, think the positive are stronger. I always respect opinions other than my own, but I hope that these opinions are formulated with an open mind and not a mind covered by selfishness.

I am supporting this issue and will be asking support from everyone I see. At the same time, I will be listening to the other side in hopes that I may even strengthen this stand.

The theme of this issue is "Do You Care?" Do you care to make your city better than it is now? Do you care to support an area that this community needs? Do you care to take the time to think carefully before you decide your opinion?

As a citizen, I am asking for your support. I am asking for the support of every reader of the paper. Since this issue, in my opinion, is so important to the community, I will be asking support from the top leaders in the state and country. Registered letters will be in the mail from the desk of Forda Birds to two men whom I greatly respect, John J. Gilligan, governor of Ohio, and Richard M. Nixon, President of the United States. I'm confident that they care.

DO YOU CARE?

January 6, 1973

1972 Was Quite a Year

During the first week in January, it always seemed appropriate to write a column recapping the previous year. I wasn't the only one who followed the practice. Journalists everywhere appeared to have the same desire. No doubt, the practice gave writers an annual evergreen topic which was easy to compose. On occasion, however, there were years that warranted a special mention. 1972 was one of them.

What made 1972 unique? First, in our area, it appeared to be the wettest year I had ever seen. During the spring, the lake was at the highest level ever recorded. On one occasion, night crawlers literally covered sections of Greenville Road as they tried to escape super-saturated ground. The fall was no better. This was the only year I can remember that many farmers weren't able to harvest their corn crops. Farmers were picking corn well into February trying to salvage what they could.

In addition to the weather, 1972 brought other significant happenings that warranted a mention. So, when some history buff looks back through old issues of the local paper, maybe some of these comments will spark them to look closer at a year that had a major impact on our own back yard.

Outdoors with Forda Birds

1972: It's History Now

1972 is a "has been" now. Many things happened, good and bad, on the local, state, national, and international scene this past year. Quite a few of these events happened on the "Forda Birds" scene as well. Let's take a look at a recap of Forda Birds, 1972.

• Readers of this column were the first to find out in 1972 that Ben Franklin didn't want the bald eagle as our national emblem. He thought that the turkey was, "a more respectable bird."

• This was the year that the April showers turned into something more. My basement and many more suddenly became swimming pools, the night crawlers covered the roads, many of the goose nests along the lake were destroyed, and the size of Lake St. Marys suddenly grew to its supposed 17,000 acres. The lake level was the highest on record.

• The Izaak Walton League cleaned up a section of the Miami & Erie Canal and planted a couple of thousand trees during 1973. Project Recycle was also born and was an immediate success.

• Environmentalists made the announcement that they had bad news and good news for the public. The good news was that by 2020 everyone in the United States would be drinking recycled sewage from the home water tap. The bad news was that there wouldn't be enough to go around.

• The 1st Annual Jaycee Canoe Races were held along the Miami & Erie Canal. This event should show that the canal is an unused recreational area, for the most part, and needs development.

• This was the year I predicted a good waterfowl hunting season. Well, the birds were here alright, but the high water that stayed with us concentrated them long the St. Marys River and later, Beaver Creek. I wasn't at either of these places until the show was over. So, Forda Bird's year for duck hunting was only fair, at best.

• September 23, 1972 was proclaimed as National Hunting & Fishing Day. This day was designed to give the sportsman a pat on the back for his work in conservation.

• This was the year that the people of St. Marys were asked to vote for or against a proposed city recreational area. The project got the support of the

White House, the Governor of our state, many service clubs, and one thousand or so voters…but failed to pass. To me, this was an inexcusable "goof" and those who voted against the issue may have saved a few dollars in taxes but in the process kicked the progress and development of our city in the tail. One thing for sure, the voters sure had me fooled.

• This was the year that may have set a new trend. In 1972, in our area, many people have the belief that there are more deer than pheasants. I'll go along with that.

• This was the year that Ken Miller at the Winchester Public Shooting Center proved to me that I couldn't play his game of "duck blind." Shooters who haven't played this game should try it. I guarantee you might like it.

• The farmers have had it rough during 1972 and continued high water and heavy rains have destroyed much of this year's grain. Some corn was never picked. Next year has to be better.

That's about the story for 1972. It has been a year I'll never forget and I hope 1973 brings more good news than bad. This column has appeared 170 times in the *Evening Leader* as of today and I hope you have enjoyed, at least, part of them. Nobody knows what "73" will bring to the outdoor world, but I plan to keep you informed as the year progresses. I enjoy doing it.

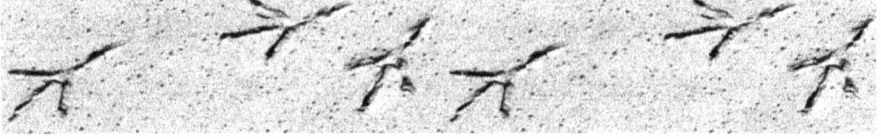

April 7, 1973

Let's Put Water Back in the Canal

In 1973, I was a firm believer that the Miami-Erie Canal could be brought back and created into a prime recreational area. However, it wasn't my idea, and again, I'll give the lion's share of the credit to Jim Kite. Jim was a township trustee at the time and had many contacts with other trustees and elected officials all along the canal. Without too much difficulty, he brought together a group of influential individuals who all thought that a canal restoration project of some sort would be good for the area.

The excitement was there, a lot of work was expended, but Jim's dream of putting water back in the canal from Lake Loramie to the St. Marys feeder never quite made it. There was one highlight, however, that needs mentioning. This group did manage to lease a mile and a half section of canal just north of Lock 8 located south of St. Marys. This was intended to be an example of how the entire canal could look. A lot of volunteer hours went into cleaning this area, and eventually, a small cement dam was constructed. The following year, with spring rains and runoff, the leased section again had water in it.

Jim and I took a canoe down this waterway, and I remember how thrilled he was. Unfortunately, it didn't take long for the water to wash around the dam, and the section was eventually abandoned.

There was some more headway made, but other obstacles got in the way and the group eventually ceased to function. The Miami-Erie Canal Development Corporation had some great ideas. Maybe the current canal group can resurrect some of them. Jim always thought the canal could be and deserved to be preserved as a monument to the men who constructed it 175 years ago. 35 years later, I still agree with him.

Outdoors with Forda Birds

Miami & Erie Canal Development: On the Move

You've read quite a bit of information about a group called the Miami & Erie Canal Development Corporation over the past months. You might know some who belong to the organization or work with it, but very likely this may seem like any other group with a fancy name.

Regardless, this group does exist and it is working and working well. Most of all, it IS different. What makes this group stand out from many of the others? First of all, it is the objectives. This group plans to clean up the section of canal from Lake Loramie to the St. Marys feeder and restore it to a prime recreational area and environmental showcase. They are not, as some people tend to believe, planning on restoring the canal to its original state and start a freight and passenger service, Even though the price of gas is going sky high, you will never be able to ride a canal boat on the entire original canal or ship your grain to Toledo or the Ohio River.

The 12 miles of dry canal to the south of St. Marys is the first step of the project, then, the remaining canal in Auglaize will be cleaned giving Auglaize County a 22 mile stretch of water, hopefully, and a 22 mile stretch of parkway, hiking trails, and other facilities.

This in a nutshell is what the organization is working to accomplish. But this in itself does not make it stand out. The goals of the group are grand and good, but the great thing about the organization is its structure. This group is a non-profit corporation and has an elected executive committee which has met every first and third Wednesday since it was formed. This meeting takes place in New Bremen and this should give you a hint as to what makes this group different. It is working in close cooperation with the Auglaize County Regional Planning Commission, the Department of Public Works, and the Department of Natural Resources. This should give you another hint as to what makes the group stand out. Have you figured it out yet? Well, this organization is different because it is working together toward a common goal with common involvement. It is working with, not pressuring the state agencies. It is working with representatives of every township and community along its boundary. And, even though it is working with all of these different factions, it is working

66

well. Can you think of another organization that is run by representatives of Salem, Noble, St. Marys, German and Jackson Townships, as well as Minster, New Bremen and St. Marys? All of these areas have their own integrity at stake, but they've thrown aside all selfish ideas and are actually working as one. To me this is amazing and if this is happening, there is no way to keep the people of Auglaize county from having something they'll be proud to talk about to their friends from out of the area. They will also share in a monument to our ancestors who had a dream and made it come true...the Miami-Erie Canal.

Just a note in passing, the Miami & Erie Development Corporation is distributing a little booklet called the Big Ditch. It is a paper back of about 50 pages made up entirely of pictures and anecdotes about the Ohio Canals. It answers some of the questions about why it was built, how it was built, and how it came to a tragic end. It's an interesting short, short course on the canal systems and easy reading for everyone.

The price of this booklet is $1.00 and the profits realized from the sale will be used to help pay organizational expenses. If you are interested in obtaining a copy, contact a member of the executive committee in your area, or drop me a line and $1.00 and I'll send you a copy the same day.

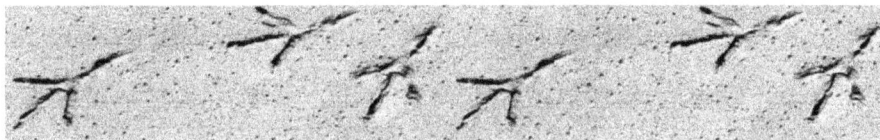

May 19, 1973

It was a Good Fishing Year

Everyone knows that fishing at Lake St. Marys seems to run in cycles. I've been fishing the lake for over 60 years now, and it always amazes me that at any given time we can have a banner fishing year then turn around and have a string of bad ones. I've yet to figure out what causes these changes, but I'm sure there are many natural and man-made factors that cause the inconsistencies. Crappie fishing seems to be the most unpredictable. One never knows how many or how big the fish will run in any given year.

Looking back over some old notes, I found that early in March of 1973 I was fishing in Rustic Haven while some ice still covered the channels. Jim Kite and I were throwing small jigs just off the edge of the ice into open water trying for some early crappies. Instead, we proceeded to catch a number of large perch, the largest I had ever seen come out of the lake. A lot of fishermen cashed in on this perch bonanza and caught perch until early June. Crappie fishing turned on, bass fishermen caught fish at will, northern pike were showing up, and the first big striped bass was reported. All in all, 1973 was a banner fishing year, and the following column reflects just how good it was.

Outdoors with Forda Birds

1973: The Year of the Fish

I don't know exactly what's happening, but something has caused the fishing in Lake St. Marys to change. Fortunately the change is for the better, and area fishermen are gathering all the benefits. Now what's been happening around the pond that would make me say that changes have been taken place? Well, first of all, probably one of the most news worthy items is the report of a super striped bass being taken from the Mercelina Park area. The fish was caught by R. Sites (Seitz), as I was told, and measured 31 inches and weighed just a bit over 14 pounds. I'm still trying to get the particulars on this catch, but I do know that it is official and the fish was entered in one of the area fishing contests. This is the first year that taking stripers is legal and it looks as if someone has scored big. While I'm thinking of monster stripers, I do hope that the fisherman who caught this prize didn't run home and cook it. First of all, it would make a dandy trophy. And secondly, the Department of Natural Resources would probably appreciate getting scale samples to determine the age of the fish and other related information. Stripers haven't been put in the lake for awhile and the stocking that was done was very limited. Now that this big striped bass has been taken, along with the many others that have been pulled out over the past few years it might be good to consider putting some more of these fish in Grand Lake St. Marys.

The 14 pound striper is new, but what really amazes me this year are the size and numbers of large mouth bass. In one channel on the north side of the lake, fishermen have told me that they have been pulling 15 to 20 good bass out nightly. Some nice bass have been taken from the Church Camp, and other areas on the south side produced bass equally well. Needless to say it's a bumper year for bass.

Last fall, I started hearing reports of nice sized perch being taken from the stone pier just west of the second swimming beach. Early this spring, fishermen started taking the same nice perch from the east bank just as soon as the ice left. Now normally, the perch fishing is done through the ice; and after the ice leaves the remaining perch fishing is slim, nil, and none. Well, this year the perch fishing is different, very much so as a matter of fact. Fishermen are catching perch off the west bank now and in large numbers. Many fishermen are using boats to find the schools of perch and are even starting to use the

Lake Erie perch rig. Many of us have taken perch from the lake and usually have been used to seeing the "mini" size. The perch that have been taken and are being taken right now aren't small. They're running on the average from 8 to 11 inches and that's a nice size perch.

Crappie fishing has been spotty until a couple of weeks ago. But, the fish are running, and almost everyone who goes out is catching enough for a meal. On the average, they're running larger. I've seen some nice catches and even wound up cleaning a mess myself a few weeks ago. I cleaned 20 nice crappies and even after skinning them had a bowl filled with just a shade under 10 pounds of meat.

A number of northern pike are being caught and quite a few in the 5 and 6 pound class are finding their way on the fisherman's stringer and into area fishing contests. The largest northern I've heard of this year has been a 9 pounder taken from the south side of the lake near Windy Point.

Well, as I said in the beginning, 1973 is going to go down as the year of the fish around here. I don't know what has brought about the change, but it's definite that a change has taken place. And I, for one, hope it stays the same.

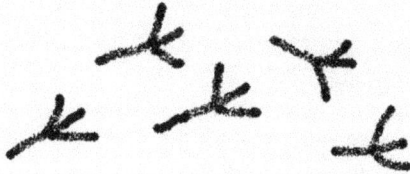

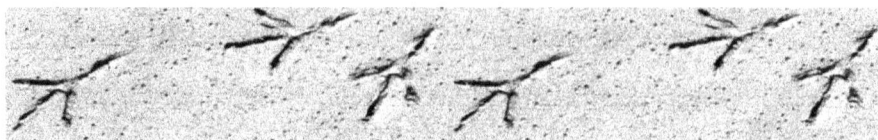

May 26, 1973

Blue Blazes

I imagine that just about every person who grew up in this neck of the woods spent time hiking along the tow path of the Miami-Erie Canal. In the fall, the area provided some decent jump shooting for ducks, and in the spring it was a great place to hunt groundhogs. Kids spent hours roaming the area carrying their air guns or rifles where targets of availability soon made them decent shots. Swimming and fishing were readily available, and more than one raft or old rowboat was launched in its waters.

When I was young, any time you visited the canal, you always got there by foot power. There was always something new to see, and this was a wild country where kids could learn to appreciate the outdoors.

With the effort to resurrect the Miami-Erie Canal a reality, some good things started to happen. The hiking potential of the canal was recognized, and people from around the state now had the chance to enjoy what the locals have enjoyed for years.

Of course, with a hiking trail designation, some of the shooting practices we enjoyed were curtailed, but that's progress, I guess. Regardless, hikers from all points of the compass could follow the blue blazes that started to appear and enjoy the outdoor experiences that most of us took for granted.

A designated state trail going through our area was a plus. Shortly after, we became part of a national trail system; one more designation that we hoped would help mark the canal as a prime recreational area that warranted developing.

Outdoors with Forda Birds

The Buckeye Trail

Eons ago, when man first came on the scene, he made his way across hills, valleys, swamps, and an occasional tar pit by simply putting one foot in front of the other. As his intelligence increased, he suddenly realized that all of this walking was for the birds and he developed the wheel. The wheel led to carts pulled by other men allowing the strongest to ride, later to carts pulled by domestic animals allowing most men to ride, and finally to carts powered by engines that allowed everyone to ride with speed and comfort.

Yes, it took many thousands of years for man to get where he is today as far as transportation is concerned. And, in the process, he has just about forgotten how to walk. Man relies on his wheels, as the present gas shortage tends to prove, and when he is threatened with the possibility of losing his major means of transportation, he panics. We are a highly developed people, but even more we're a highly mobile people. Our country is laced with thousands and thousands of miles of super highways, and the future seems to tell us that we're going to have many more miles before it's all finished. We are a nation that is bound to the wheel and everyone will probably agree that this is a good idea. Well, maybe almost everyone!

I said maybe because there are many people around this country and in this state, for that matter, who have realized that there is a great deal of merit to using the God given method of transportation, the feet. Who are these people? Well, they're just like you and me and most of them own a car. The only difference is that they are people who suddenly realized that even though they had nice cars and cross country highways, these roads only covered point to point and usually led nowhere except to a place similar to the one they left. These people realized there were many places in this country that couldn't be seen from the road and could only be seen by parking the car and taking off cross country. Thus the hiker was born. The members of Buckeye Trail Association are from all walks of life, and they simply enjoy getting off the beaten path and seeing much of the country that they would otherwise have missed. They are also a group of people who want to share what they have found out and therefore formed an organization back in 1959 to establish a series of trails across the state for anyone to walk. We are now part of this trail.

Last week, members of the Buckeye Trails Association came to St. Marys and traveled the entire area of the Miami-Erie Canal from Ft. Loramie to Spencerville with the purpose of including it in their approximately 900 miles. The trail as it stands today starts on the shores of Lake Erie at the eastern edge of Ohio and follows fairly close the contour of the state until it reaches Cincinnati. It then heads north until Lockington and then stops. After the board met here last Saturday, they decided to formally include the section of canal from St. Marys through Spencerville as part of the Buckeye Trail with plans for the future development of the trail from Ft. Loramie to St. Marys.

Now what does this mean? Well, first of all, it means that people who enjoy hiking can now start at St. Marys at the City Parking lot and by following a series of little blue marks that will soon be placed, follow a trail that will take them to the areas not available by road and share in some of the wonders that nature has to offer. It also means that many of the hikers around Ohio and neighboring states will come to St. Marys and hike an area that only the locals knew about but seldom appreciated. All in all, the establishment of a trail through this area is a good addition. The Buckeye Trail Association does not own any of the land along the trail but simply functions as an organizing body similar to the Miami-Erie Canal Development Corporation.

In cooperation with various local, county, and state governmental agencies, they mark off areas that are available both physically and legally. Then they make maps of these areas and provide them to hikers. A local person is then put in charge of the trail section and is responsible for the blue blazes that are posted and the general appearance and usage. He is not a maintenance man and does not pick up garbage or mow grass. His job is to help the hikers enjoy the trail and handle any comments and suggestions they might have.

Regardless, the trail is now officially in existence and hopefully will be extended to the south in the future. So, if you get the urge to take a walk, you now have a place to go—some 22 miles if you feel up to it. If you have any questions about the Buckeye Trails Association, drop down to the City Park during the Sesquicentennial. Representatives will be there in the big tent, along with the Miami-Erie Canal Corporation, the Izaak Walton League, and the Ohio Division of Wildlife. Someone will be happy to answer your questions.

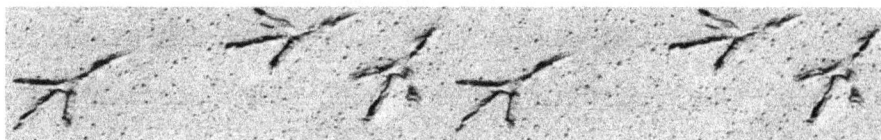

June 30, 1973

Outdoors with Forda Birds

The North Country Trail

As you may have read yesterday in the *Evening Leader*, a meeting was held at Memorial High School to discuss a potential addition to the National Trails System. The new trail, called the North Country Trail, would pass in part through our area with the Miami-Erie Canal as the center of the trail corridor.

Now, this whole idea is just in the initial planning stages, but, it would appear that if the feeling of the other meetings held in the states included had the same atmosphere and positive feelings toward this venture, the trail would someday be a reality.

One of the high points of the meeting was a formal statement presented by Richard Ballenger, president of the Miami-Erie Canal Development Corporation. His remarks explaining the structure of the organization, its accomplishments, and its plans added greatly to the overall meeting. At the end of the meeting, a slide presentation narrated by Jim Kite gave everyone the feeling that this area was ready, willing, and able to do its fair share in promoting outdoor recreational facilities in the area.

Mr. Ballenger related that the canal organization since its formation in May, 1972, had initiated a feasibility study through the Auglaize County Regional Planning commission. He reported that members of the group had given presentations at more than 50 events during the year. He also mentioned that the group had endorsed and heavily supported legislation dealing with the canal and was working closely with the Johnny Appleseed Metropolitan Park District of Allen County and Buckeye Trails Inc. of Columbus, Ohio.

Much of the work of the organization has been leg work and paper work. Another point that was made in this formal statement, however, should give those of you who are asking when actual work will begin, an answer.

It was mentioned that a lease had been obtained from the Department of Public Works, State of Ohio, through St. Marys Township to start actual cleanup with volunteer help. The lease covers canal land south of St. Marys that extends some 1.5 miles in length. Actual work on this section of land will begin this fall, and it is expected that by December a good start will have been made in creating a showplace for everyone to enjoy.

Yes, the Miami-Erie Canal Development Corporation is just a little over one year old. It's young, but it's producing and that's all one can ask. It's producing because the canal is a good project. Even more than that, it's producing because a group of people representing every community and township along the way are making it work by working together.

I don't know what the future holds for this project. As an interested citizen I can only hope that the total plans, as they are being visualized, come to completion. This project needs your help and moral support. Who knows, maybe someday when your kids and grandkids ask you about the big ditch, you can tell them what is used to be like in the "70's" before it was restored to a thing of beauty.

Annual Goose Banding Completed

The annual wild goose banding at the Mercer County Wildlife Area was completed this past Thursday. Unlike last year, because of the flood conditions, an extremely good hatch of birds was banded. According to records, 1845 new bands were put out and approximately 1700 of these birds were hatched here this season. Another estimated 500 birds could not be captured for this purpose.

Six hundred birds were removed from the area and taken to Killdear Plains and Crane Creek. This is not a new move since birds have been supplied to these areas from Mercer County for the past couple of years.

Regardless, the results of the banding give a glimmer of hope to the waterfowl hunter. He'll at least have an additional 1100 area birds to chase when opening day rolls around this October.

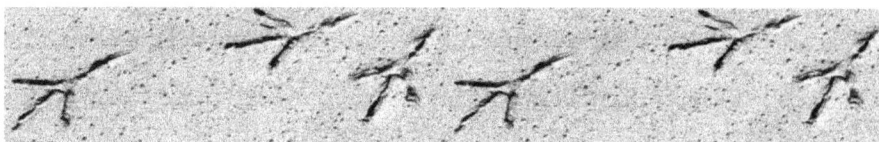

July 21, 1973

It's Time to License Boaters

I started my boating career some 60 years ago when my dad began teaching me the fine art of rowing a boat. It didn't take long before I could handle myself in fairly rough water always pushing the oars rather than pulling them. I was probably 12 when I got my first ride in a motor boat. It was a 14 foot aluminum runabout with a 25 horsepower engine. It was also supposed to be the fastest boat on the lake at the time. The second fastest boat on the lake had twin 15 horsepower engines and was made of wood. The rest is history.

It didn't take long before boating popularity began growing by leaps and bounds. Credit became a way of life and was easy to get. Marinas were dealing. The motor sizes increased as boaters sought the excitement of speed. Fishing boats appeared stressing not only comfort and efficiency but speed as well. Sailboats started regaining popularity. Then came the infamous Jet Ski. Heavy weekends found thousands of people on the water who had little knowledge about the sport of boating other than it was fun. There were few laws on the books to help keep boaters safe and little enforcement in the beginning. Anyone could drive any boat at any age, and that spelled trouble.

It was time for boating education. It was also evident that some day, a boating license would become a reality. The education part developed quickly when the Lima Power Squadron started offering free courses at the St. Marys Boat Club. I took a number of them, and learned a great deal. If nothing more, I learned to respect the water, respect my boat, and respect my fellow boaters. Today, mandatory boating training is required for all new boaters. I think that's a good thing, and it was seriously talked about around here long before it became a reality.

Outdoors with Forda Birds

Watercraft Education: Is it Necessary?

I spend a great deal of time around and on lakes, and one thing that always amazes me is the number of boats that are always around. I imagine that the number of boats that are registered in the immediate area would number in the thousands and that would still only represent a percentage of the actual number of boats that travel our waterways, primarily Lake St. Marys.

Since there are many boats and boat owners in our area, I've made a few observations that appear to be fair general statements. I've noticed that most boat owners are fun-loving people who enjoy their sport. They enjoy their sport, they're friendly, and they're looking for an exciting, interesting, "good time" on the lake.

I've also noticed that the number of boat owners is increasing and the only deterrent to becoming a boat owner is money. Regardless of the type of watercraft, be it canoe, rowboat, sailboat, or battleship, the price that is paid also appears to give to the new owner an instant knowledge about watercraft operation. It appears this way, but it's false. Just because a person owns a boat doesn't mean that he's qualified to take it out on the water. It might sound ridiculous, but that's exactly what's happening. Many boaters are buying their first boat and hitting the water with no more knowledge of what they're doing than the man in the moon.

Now, there was a time when going out in a boat required little knowledge, and this knowledge could be obtained in a short time by experience. This learning method of "flying by the seat of your pants" was relatively safe. A few years ago, there weren't many boats around compared to today's vast numbers. The power of engines was relatively limited and too much speed was never a safety consideration. Today, however, the situation is different and all of the factors that made boating safe by nature are no longer present. Today, the number of boats and boaters are increasing at an enormous rate. Designs of watercraft and engine power are such that speed is bordering close to highway speed. These factors make boating more dangerous today than it was 20 years ago.

Yes, boating is more dangerous today, but it doesn't have to be that way. The problem could be greatly reduced if the boater took the time and learned the rules and knowledge that go hand in hand with safe boat handling. Now, boaters who are reading this may think what I'm saying is all wet. But, let's look at one comparison and maybe a few minds can be changed. Way back when, manned flight was something that many people said would never happen. These critics were wrong and man did fly. During the infancy of powered flight, men learned to fly by flying. They learned by experience and some didn't learn fast enough. As flying became more sophisticated and the number of planes increased, man realized that there was a great deal of knowledge that had to be learned before flying became safe. A man could no longer buy a plane, hop in the cockpit, start the engine, and hope for the best because if he didn't kill himself, he might kill somebody else.

This country has reached the same stage in boating, and boaters who are using sophisticated equipment today can no longer start their engine and hope for the best. Today, the inexperienced boater can easily kill himself (and he does), or even worse kill someone else.

I've made my case and now I'd like to make a proposition to all the boaters in the area. A couple of days ago, I sat down and talked with Jim French and Jim Hopewell who are with the Division of Watercraft, Department of Natural Resources. These men work in enforcement and education and service some 21 counties in the state. We discussed the problems of boating, and came up with the idea that many boaters might be interested in taking a training course in watercraft operation. We tossed around such topics as accidents and how to avoid them, maintenance of equipment, required equipment and its use, laws and regulations, rules of the road, safety tips, trailering, basic weather, and many others. At the end of our conversation, it was decided that a course covering these topics should be offered if boaters were interested. The course would be offered at Lake St. Marys during the fall and winter months for little if any cost. So, people who took this training would be able to hit the water next spring with confidence in themselves and in their equipment.

This is the idea that we had and whether it ever gets to be more than an idea is up to the area boaters. What I need is your response to the idea. If you're interested in this type of training, drop me a line at the *Evening Leader*. If you're like me and can't find the time to write, call the Division of Parks Office, 394-3611 and give them your comments.

The theory of watercraft training is based on the assumption that you owe it to yourself, your family, and to the other boater to know what you're doing when you get in your watercraft and take off across the water. Many boaters do know what they are doing, but many do not. All could know more. Do you agree?

October 13, 1973

"Pets and plants aren't usually harmed."

I lost my little sister to cancer. She was 43 years old. There was no family history of the disease, and no way to determine what caused it. It just happened. Having said that, I do know her husband spent a lot of time salmon fishing in Lake Michigan, and they ate his catch with regularity thinking it was a healthy food. Unfortunately, it was later discovered that these fish carried high concentrations of PCBs, a known carcinogen.

DDT was a popular poison used for years but was finally banned in 1972. Substitute poisons were then used and justified with a cavalier attitude that although they might be harmful, one wouldn't know about it for a long time. There were proponents of popular pesticides that volunteered to drink the poison straight from the bottle. I always thought this to be a bit radical, and after various risk assessments were eventually developed, I don't think anyone in their right mind would take such a drastic step to prove a point.

Regardless, there wasn't much of an outcry from the people when St. Marys got a dose of dieldrin and aldrin to control the Japanese beetle. After all, those of us who are a bit older can remember the annual summer spraying of DDT to control mosquitoes before it was banned. It didn't seem to hurt us then. Unfortunately, there is a distinct possibility that it affected a lot of people down the road.

I read *Silent Spring* in the late 1960s and bought into Rachel Carson's conclusions. Because of that book, I thought the following column was warranted. It wasn't long before we found out that there were thousands of tons of various chemicals in our environment that could eventually kill us. Now, everyone is aware of the conditions or should be.

Outdoors with Forda Birds

Pesticides in St. Marys

Silent Spring, a now famous book by Rachel Carson, first appeared in print over ten years ago. It dealt with and presented a rather unsavory picture of what manmade pollutants are doing to our environment. I have read the book, mentioned it in this column almost four years ago, and now suggest that every person of this community, especially those who have just had their property treated with pesticides, read it.

This past week, areas of our community were treated with the chemicals dieldrin and aldrin by personnel of the Ohio Department of Agriculture and the U.S. Department of Agriculture. The purpose of this treatment was to control the Japanese beetle. Now, this statement in itself does not sound very earth shattering, but to me it is and should be to all of you.

Ever since I began writing this column some four years ago, I began to be exposed to literature concerning all aspects of the outdoors. I've read pages and pages about hunting, fishing, camping, boating, and who knows what else. I've also read quite a bit about pesticides and their relationship to our ecosystem. It is from this reading and other sources that made me concerned when I heard that the chemicals dieldrin and aldrin were being spread about the community.

I've been spinning my wheels all week trying to figure out how to put this column together since my qualifications to speak about pesticides are not much better than many other people. On top of that, I have a responsibility to you, the reader, to present an unemotional, objective report on controversial issues. And, that type of report is extremely difficult, maybe impossible.

Regardless, here is some information that I've gathered this past week, and some questions that I have the right to ask concerning this situation.

First of all, since my knowledge of pesticides is rather slim, I sought some advice and information from a qualified chemist who works at a nearby laboratory, and a Professor of Biology at the Wright State University Branch. Their reactions to this pesticide treatment were extremely negative. Now that you know my background, you can give the following comments any degree of credibility you wish.

Dieldrin and aldrin are pesticides called chlorinated hydrocarbons and are relatives of DDT. One of the most important characteristics of these chemicals is that it is persistent and offers excellent residual activity. In plain words, these chemicals hang around for a long time in the soil, in some cases for more than ten years. They have been shown to have low acute toxicity in humans. That means you can take rather large doses of this chemical without immediate ill effects. Research has shown, however, that concentrations of chlorinated hydrocarbons were greater in patients who died from cerebral hemorrhage, cirrhosis of the liver, cancer, and other various illnesses. All of us have chlorinated hydrocarbons in our systems. These residuals rest in their potency and are stored in our bodies. As the amounts increase, so do the dangers to our health.

What about immediate effects of the pesticides in question? These chemicals are extremely dangerous to all forms of animal life until they are taken into the ground. The notice received by residents of St. Marys states that, "pets and plants are not usually harmed, except for such grass eating animals as rabbits, which should be confined until the area is wet down by rain or hosed," One of the questions that concern me is that many animals besides rabbits have been known to eat grass. Pets, such as cats, walk through most lawns in town and sometimes during the day lick their paws. Children play in many yards throughout the city and could take undue amounts of this chemical into their systems.

Once the chemical is in the soil, things begin to happen to the natural balance. Night crawlers are necessary for a healthy lawn and they ingest this pesticide. A robin comes along and eats maybe ten worms until he has enough chemical to cause his end. Here's another example of how this chemical works. If you follow a rule of thumb that says a given level in a food chain will rarely be more than 1/10 the weight of the organism at the next lower level, you can come up with these figures. For every 1,000 pounds of grass, one can expect 100 pounds of cow. And, for every 100 pounds of cow one can expect 10 pounds of man. If this grass contained one part per million of a pesticide, how many parts per million would a man ingest into his system at the end of the chain?

Are dieldrin and aldrin harmful? The best answer I can determine is, "Compared to what." It's a difficult question to answer. Yet, just because you are alive to renew your driver's license doesn't mean that driving on the nation's highways is safe,

Regardless, the pesticides have been put down in our city by agencies that have the authority under a section of the Ohio Revised Code, and residents have been assured that the chemicals are safe. My last question then is, if these chemicals are so safe, why do the people who are applying it wear masks? I guess we'll find out one of these years.

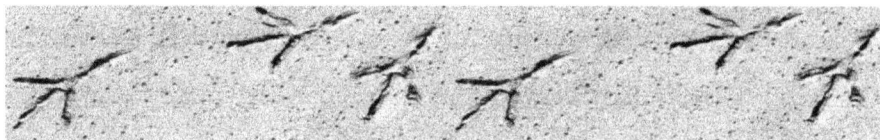

January 19, 1974

Where's the Gas?

1973 was an interesting year for gasoline consumers. We had a shortage of crude oil and of gasoline. Some leaders in the oil industry seemed to enjoy telling their gloom and doom scenarios. One statement that I recall focused on the fact that our entire supply of raw crude oil would be depleted in 30 years.

Regardless, gasoline was hard to get from time to time. I recall heading to Michigan and carrying extra gas in my boat in case I ran out. I do remember that while driving north throughout the night, I never came across an open gas station until I was well north of Jackson, Michigan.

Speed limits were reduced to 55 and gasoline stations were only open six days a week. Long lines waited at the pumps, and in some cases, the amount of purchase was limited. We thought it was terrible that some profiteering gas station owners were charging $2.00 a gallon for gas.

Sportsmen were getting prepared to take a serious hit. Motor homes would be put up on blocks, boats would be kept in storage, and outdoor recreation as we knew it would cease to exist.

For whatever reason, I never heard of anyone who lost a day on the water because of a gasoline shortage. Motor homes still took to the roads. Somehow, gasoline supplies became plentiful again.

As I look back at 2008 and the $4.00 a gallon gasoline many of us had to purchase, I wonder if the same thing isn't happening again. Just like in the 1970s, I'm sure there are people making billions of dollars by manipulating the oil market. Maybe this time around, the American people will be wise enough to realize that oil is a nonrenewable resource. If we'd have gotten the hint 35 years ago, all of us might now be plugging our electric cars in at night or simply fueling them with tap water.

Outdoors with Forda Birds

Americans Adjust to a Crisis

I've always been taught, told, and believed that the American people had the ability to rise as a group in the face of adversity. Since our revolution and declaration of independence to present days, people from every walk of life have stopped what they were doing and adjusted their way of life to solve a national crisis.

During WW II, women kept the home front operating and took over the manufacture of war materials while their men went to war. Almost all forms of produce and raw materials came under rationing, and the American people lived under these restrictions without too much difficulty. The reason? Everyone was united under a common, obvious cause, the elimination of unjust aggression.

Today we are in the middle of another crisis that has consequences as serious, if not more serious, than the Second World War. Since it's not as obvious as the War, people are having a bit of trouble realizing that a crisis does exist. During the war, many fathers, sons, and husbands lost their lives…this brought the meaning of crisis home. As far as our energy crisis is concerned, people can still get gasoline, we appear to have more crude oil in storage than we had last year, rumors of oil company conspiracy are everywhere, and Ralph Nader is attacking the problem as strong-armed robbery.

I'm like many other people in this country when I say that something doesn't seem right. I, like many other people in this country, don't have the knowledge or background to even make an intelligent judgment. Regardless, the big wigs in government and the oil industry say we are short of fuel and we have to believe it. After all, they all make more money that I do a year, so they might be right. How's that for logic! Even though I might not be smart enough to tell the status of our energy, I think I am smart enough to see the obvious. And, the obvious tells me that anytime you produce something from raw materials, the supply of the raw materials decrease. I don't know if we are in the middle of a real fuel shortage right now, but I do feel that if we continue to use raw materials at the same alarming rates we are now, the American people are, someday, going to be faced with a crisis even worse than what we have in 1974.

The energy crisis has already started taking its toll from the industries. Recreational areas are being extremely hard hit. I noticed the other day that Trotwood Trailers went out of business. Many of the small boat manufacturers that use fiberglass have had to close their doors because of lack of fiberglass. Recreational vehicles are taking a beating and many of the new plush campgrounds along with them.

I received a release from an outfit called Outdoor Resorts. It seems to me that out of desperation they have come up with the following plan. The name of the plan: "Turn off Your Furnace, Turn on the Florida Sun." The program has three primary purposes:

1. A free telephone service to advise campers about the availability of gasoline.

2. A special $99 per month rate (vs. the normal $180) at the 1000-site resort at Orlando. The resort has a 176 acre lake for sailing or fishing, a nine-hole golf course, Olympic size pool, tennis courts, horseshoe pits, and many other facilities for easy camping. With that type of investment it appears they need any money they can get to make the interest payments.

3. This resort is making a money back guarantee at all of their Florida resorts. If campers are not satisfied with the facilities after the first night, they get their money back.

Now that sounds nice and friendly, but I've yet to see anyone in the business of making money give it away.

I've come on pretty hard against this particular operation simply because it appears to be a signal of things to come. We have a crisis in this country that calls for a total effort. This effort will never materialize if industry, governments, and the people try to take advantage of this situation to make a buck. One thing for sure, it's going to be interesting to watch what goes on in this old world the next few months.

January 24, 1974

Five Dollars a Shot

When I was a kid and started buying my own shotgun shells, I seldom could afford to buy a whole box. Fortunately, the local hardware store sold broken boxes. Small game loads were a nickel a piece, and the high velocity shells we used for ducks cost a dime. Lead was cheap, and making lead shot was inexpensive and easy to do. There was no doubt that the price of scattergun ammunition was a bargain.

Waterfowl management is a major issue with the Fish & Wildlife Service, and when some obscure research suddenly revealed negative effects of lead shot, action was called for. It was discovered that ducks were ingesting spent lead shot in marsh lands and were dying from lead poisoning. Further research estimated that possible annual duck losses numbered in the millions. Once these numbers were validated, it was proposed that lead shot be outlawed for waterfowl hunting. Coming up with an alternative material became a problem. Ammunition manufacturers scrambled to develop a material that had the weight of lead and was as easy to produce. The initial results failed on both counts. The best material they could come up with was steel, and making it into shot was expensive. Also, the ballistics of steel was nowhere near that of lead.

The debate started immediately when hunters found out that shells they didn't like and were forced to use would cost them and additional 30 to 40 percent. Regardless, the die was cast and steel became the required waterfowl shot across the entire country.

Since then, the ammunition industry has worked to develop non-toxic heavy shot to replace lead. In 2009, there are many heavy shots on the market that are as good as lead, if not better. There are two major problems with these premium shotgun shells. First, the best of the best can cost five dollars a shot. Second, they don't make a hunter any better at hitting his target.

Steel shot had a major impact on the shotgun shell industry. That's why I wrote the following column and why it warrants a mention in this volume.

Outdoors with Forda Birds

Iron Shot in "76"?

Over the years, the sport of waterfowl hunting has become ultra complicated. It must have been great back in the days of the market hunter when the limits were measured in weight instead of birds and the season was based on when the birds arrived in the area. But, those days are gone and good riddance.

Today, this sport of millions has become a highly complicated, technical sport because of the massive amounts of regulations that are demanded by the structure. Management is a primary concern of the Department of Interior, as well as the harvesting (hunting) itself. Regardless, hunters are faced with bag limits, point systems, time regulations, space regulations, and regulations covering everything else.

One of the newest proposed pieces of legislation deals with the use of iron shot. A few years ago, studies showed that lead shot was killing a great number of waterfowl. It seemed that the birds were picking up this shot as they fed, and its ingestion caused paralysis and eventually death. How many birds did this affect? Some estimates ranged as high as three million birds a year, an alarming rate.

Because of this problem, a lead shot substitute was requested and all ammunition companies began to work on the problems. The result of their research was a soft iron shot that would eliminate this waste of waterfowl caused by the toxic lead. When this shot was finally announced as having been satisfactorily developed, the Department of the Interior announced a time table stating that it would be used in the Atlantic Flyway during the 1974 season and then would be adopted nation wide during the 1975 season.

This announcement brought cries of protests from everyone. The waterfowl hunter was upset because the ammunition was not as "good" as lead and besides that, it would cost two or three dollars more a box. The ammunition dealers were upset because it was hard to produce, could possibly damage firearms, and called for a major expenditure in new equipment. Other people involved in this situation questioned the fact that a problem existed, and if one did, its magnitude. Others purported studies that proved iron shot caused more crippling than its counterpart. The protestors won out and for awhile the question of iron shot's use in waterfowl was almost forgotten.

But, iron shot is back today, and its use in the future is almost guaranteed. The National Wildlife Federation has stated that the problem of lead shot poisoning waterfowl will continue to grow as the concentrations of hunting lands increase. To make their point, they are preparing an injunction against the Department of Interior to prevent hunters from using a toxic substance on marsh lands. The government, in turn, is listening and it appears that iron shot will be mandatory by 1976, possibly in 1975. The groundwork has been put down and an environmental impact study has been prepared. This is the last step before a decision is made.

So, it looks like waterfowl hunters will again have to adjust. They'll have to watch their shooting and stop taking all of those wild shots. If nothing more, the additional cost of ammunition should control their shooting habits. Not only will they have to control their shooting, but they will also have to take this situation in stride for the betterment of waterfowl hunters everywhere. Conservationists across the country will be looking to see how the waterfowl hunter responds to this situation. If he groans and moans, many will think that all the waterfowl hunter is concerned about is killing waterfowl. If he responds positively, conservationists will have to believe that we are concerned about our waterfowl populations and intend to make sure that our sport is around for many, many years.

March 23, 1974

What the Future Holds

Thirty-five years ago, after I had written this column for a few years, I started developing a feeling for this area that I never had before. I was watching things more closely than I usually do, and what I saw wasn't always very pleasant. Looking around my outdoor world and after seeing many other parts of the country, I had a pretty good idea of how I wanted development to take place. I saw a greater potential for Lake St. Marys, the Miami-Erie Canal, and other outdoor spots that made this area so unique.

At the same time, I saw many of the obstacles that could hinder this grand scheme I envisioned. Lack of money was a major concern. Who was willing to spend the dollars it would take to make this area a premier outdoor recreational site? Next, was greed. For example, there was and is a lot of money to be made from buying, selling, and developing lake property. It seemed to me that these practices were in no way compatible with prudent recreational development. Finally, I learned to believe that politics and politicians seldom did anything for merit alone. So, I became cynical at a very young age when it suddenly dawned on me that governments are run by people who are bought and sold. One can't become a successful politician without owing somebody something.

Today, I can sit back, sip a beer, and imagine what our area will look like in 10, 50, or 100 years. I know what I want to see, but the vision always has a bad side. As I drive around the lake and surrounding farm country, I see many changes. Most would call it progress. I don't look at it that way.

Think about it. Our outdoor recreational area drew the people, and the people destroyed the area in the process. If that pattern continues, it doesn't create a very pretty picture for the future.

Outdoors with Forda Birds

Time to Prophesy

After a person has had his hand on the pulse of the outdoors for awhile, he tends to see trends and ideas come to light. He doesn't, however, get the entire picture, isn't exposed to all sides, and seldom can distinguish the whole truth. But, he still develops feelings and opinions, sometimes formed by the brain, usually formed by the gut.

The other night, I happened to be thinking about our area, its potential, and what it would be like in the next ten years or so. It's fun to brainstorm, sometimes, and in the process you see things you like and things you don't like. Regardless, I'd like to share some of the things I saw, and you figure out if they're good news or bad news.

Lake St. Marys: To be realistic, Lake St. Marys is a problem lake and costly to maintain. It's shallow, dirty most of the time, and especially treacherous to boaters. Yet, it is a well used recreational area with potential and a most important asset to the area. Funds to keep this lake in order are hard to come by, and because of this, for example, dredging has been slowed down. Dredging, of course, is what gives this lake a chance, and if this operation is not completely restored, problems will soon get out of hand. If money is made available, I see a different lake in the future. A series of islands will have been constructed over the next ten years, and natural areas as well as formal park areas will be developed on what is now leased land. A major park will be developed on the west side of the lake that will probably be even larger than the one on the east shore. If money isn't made available, I can also see a person driving down the east bank road, looking across the country side to the west, and seeing one great big corn field divided by cheap, damp, housing developments. Doesn't sound possible? Well, give the developers a chance.

Miami-Erie Canal: The canal? Well, it is quite obvious to most who see the canal that a great recreational potential is present. Interested citizens have taken an interest and over the past couple of years have made a good start. But, after many hours of labor, the future of the canal as a recreational area rests on a piece of legislation called HB 829. If the legislation is passed, I can someday see a beautiful parkway of some 35 miles running through the area giving thousands of people countless hours of enjoyment. If this legislation goes the way it appears to be going, if this area continues to be ignored by the state, and if the political pull continues to funnel the bulk of funds to the metropolitan areas, the Miami-Erie Canal will continue to be the garbage dump it is today.

Mercer County Waterfowl Refuge: Of course, I have a soft spot in my head and heart for this place. A couple of years ago all sorts of problems came up concerning this area and, I feel, marked the things to come. My prediction is that this area will never grow in size and will even have trouble maintaining its present level as politicians and developers go about their business. In my opinion, the waterfowl refuge in Mercer County will be surrounded by development in the next ten years and in following years be strangled completely out of existence. I hope I saw the wrong picture.

I've tried to give a little insight into three of the most important areas we have. Be rest assured that I'm just guessing, but my guesses are based on more than just some dusty crystal ball, And, with that in mind, I'll make one more prophesy.

Outdoors with Forda Birds: The only major change one might find in this column over the next ten years, if it's still around, is that the writer will have a tendency to show increased frustration and bitterness as he watches the leaders of this state and nation stumbling along, using their mouths instead of their conscience to do the job they have been chosen to do. What will hurt even more is that most people will still probably be letting them get away with it.

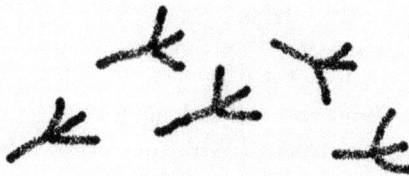

July 20, 1974

Monster Fish

In April of 1965, I was in the Army at San Antonio, Texas trying to learn something about my job. Because of the nature of the school, I had some free time and spent most of it at a lake where the military provided me with a small mobile home and a fishing boat for the weekend. Total cost of the amenities was $8, if I remember correctly. I caught a lot of fish and ate a lot of fish. It was quite a deal. I also caught the biggest fish of my life, a 14 pound flathead catfish.

Somewhere I have a picture of me holding up this catch, and although this particular fish had to be one of the ugliest critters on the planet, it looked pretty good to me at the moment. I've hooked larger flatheads during my lifetime, but never managed to land another one. The gear I used wasn't strong enough to handle these big fish. Although as ugly as a mud fence, I learned to appreciate the raw power of these monsters. They're a killing machine when they want to be, and at the same time, bigger fish might lounge in a deep hole not eating for a week or longer.

I was excited when I heard that flathead catfish were released in Lake St. Marys. The fish were about two inches long, and it didn't take much time for them to start growing and feeding. With the forage fish we have in the lake, there was no doubt in my mind that some monster catfish would soon make the fishing scene.

Today, an occasional big flathead is caught, but I'm sure more could be landed if fishermen went after them specifically. I'm also sure that a number of flatheads have broken a line or a pole without the fisherman ever seeing what was on the other end.

9,000 flathead catfish were released in August of 1973. Who knows how many there are now or how big Lake St. Marys flatheads are today. It would be exciting for any fisherman to tangle with a monster, and that's a definite possibility.

Outdoors with Forda Birds

Flathead Catfish

A number of years ago when I was living in Kansas, I had the opportunity to do quite a bit of fishing. Contrary to common belief, there is water in Kansas and much of it contains top flight fishing. Walleye fishing was the "in thing" in certain parts of Tuttle Creek Lake and limit catches were quite common if you knew where to go.

It was while I was fishing for walleye that I had my first meeting with a monster flathead catfish. I was fishing a yellow doll fly trailed by a juicy night crawler when the big fish hit. I knew immediately that it wasn't one of the large crappies we had been taking all afternoon, or one of the good walleye that occasionally struck. This was a big fish and had the fighting spirit of a giant log. The fish would swim around in lazy circles for awhile then slowly settle to the bottom and rest. I put all kinds of strain on the fish and he never moved. Finally he made up his mind that sitting on the bottom was a waste of time so he circled a bit longer and then headed for the surface. As the big fish came to the top of the water, my fishing partner, a barber from Manhattan hollered, "Shovel!" I wondered what he wanted with a shovel at a time like this and then suddenly realized that he was talking about a shovelhead catfish, known more commonly as flathead.

To make a long story short, the fish was estimated to weigh 60 pounds and as we watched it resting on the surface, it made one sluggish flip of the tail and headed for the bottom. This "fight" lasted for most of an hour with the fish taking ten minute breathers about every 20 minutes. When it decided to go to the bottom of the pool and sit, an explosive charge couldn't begin to hold it. At the end, the line finally parted and the fish went back to his home somewhere in the lake, not even bothered by the experience.

That is the flathead for you. Why mention these fish? The primary reason is that some 9000 of these creatures were stocked last August in Lake St. Marys. Reports I've recently received tell me that some of these fish are now being caught and are running 15 and 16 inches in length. This is fantastic growth since they were only 1 ½ inches when they were stocked.

All along the Mississippi River Valley clear down to Mexico the flathead is a popular fish with the fishermen. He is a large fish with the average size running between 3 and 4 pounds. But, some of these fish have been weighed in at 100 pounds.

He's not an attractive fish, but it appears that he is here in the lake and doing well. One thing for sure, if he continues to grow at the rate reported, it won't be too many years before someone hooks a 40, 50, or 60, or even a 100 pounder. I don't know how long this will take, but the fisherman who tangles with this giant, stubborn overgrown bullhead had better be using a pool cue rigged with rope or he won't stand much of a chance. As they used to say on TV, "No brag, just fact."

December 28, 1974

It Seemed Significant at the Time

As I look back over 40 years of writing outdoor columns, I noticed that I selected certain years as being more significant than others. All of them, however, were unique in their own way. 1974 had too many incidents to be ignored. First, there was the gasoline shortage that threw the public into panic. Somehow, that was resolved, and an additional 30 years of gasoline- guzzling cars cruised our highways.

Anti-hunting groups became more prevalent backed by funds gained from people who were either ignorant or duped. I remember receiving a flyer from California from a woman who had started an organization called STS. Evidently, she had heard shooting near her home and was shocked to hear that it came from a skeet field. With the amount of shooting she heard, there was no doubt in her mind that all of the skeet in the area would be killed. Her organization was designed to stop this slaughter. Thus the name: STS, Save the Skeet. For those of you who don't know, skeet is a shooting game that uses clay targets. Was the woman just plain stupid or running a scam? I gave her more credit than she deserved and declared her a con artist, albeit a poor one.

Other incidents occurred in 1974 that, if nothing more, had an impact on me. I guess that's why I included the following piece in this first volume of significant columns. It might have been considered a "fluff" piece to end the year, but those recorded happenings signaled inevitable future events, many of which turned out to be even more monumental.

Outdoors with Forda Birds

The Way It Was: 1974

Another New Year is about to begin. For some, the old year has been a good one, for others, not so good. And, some haven't really given it much thought. Regardless, if you aren't too sure what type of year 1974 was, here's a recap of some of the more interesting things that happened...at least as far as the outdoors go.

Probably the biggest story to hit the outdoor news was the energy crisis. Of course, it hit the country in more ways than just recreation, but since recreation is such a big business, the kick was felt in more ways than one. Gasoline shortages across the country created long lines at the pumps and made the recreation oriented business cringe with the inevitable disaster. Camping trailer sales slowed to a crawl in many areas and motor homes were an almost "no-no." Some manufacturers closed their doors while others were thankful for their companies' diversification. Boating related industries surveyed their $4 billion dollar industry and predicted lean "pickens."

But, something happened and we did have gasoline to run our cars. We could get gas for the family boat or camper. And, the slogan, "Turn off your furnace, turn on the Florida sun," died a slow death. In spite of the big gas scare, in spite of the fact that we are short of gasoline, in spite of the fact that we're paying a great deal more, the outdoorsman moved around the country as usual and still managed to spend 14 per cent of his income on recreation.

At the beginning of last year I said that the anti-hunting groups would gain in strength and start to make themselves heard cross the country. They did, and as a result, for example, the 1974 waterfowl season was almost stopped by court action. Expect to hear more from these groups in 1975 and remember that their great philosophy appears to be, "When man wantonly destroys the works of God, he is called a sportsman."

The Miami-Erie Canal project was reported, from time to time, to be on the move. A letter received by the Director of the Department of Natural Resources in late April stated, Very soon the Department will be taking direct action to maintain and preserve the corridor." Since Governor Gilligan lost by a nose in November and Director Nye was summarily put out to pasture, "very soon" might be changed to, "one of these days." Of course, that's how it happened in 1974 and I still have hopes that things will be looking up early in 1975.

Other bits of interest rest around the sport of fishing. Fishermen had an outstanding year for crappies in Lake St. Marys. A record striper was taken from the lake. Some 9000 flathead catfish were stocked in August 1973 and some 14 inch fish were reported caught last summer. Around 400 stripers, approximately eight inches in length, were released this year. And, last but probably the most important, the lake was low all summer long as this area suffered one of the longest, driest periods on record,.

A series called, "It's In Your Own Backyard" was run in the *Leader* this past summer and from time to time will reappear. Gun legislation made its way into the spotlight but thankfully common sense ruled the outcome. Forda Birds was five years old in October and my little girl was 3. She, by the way, caught her first fish last August.

All in all, I have to mark 1974 down in the books as a good one. Oh, there were some problems but that only makes life interesting. Maybe I'll just change my statement and say that if 1974 wasn't a good year, at least it was an interesting one. What is in store for "75"? I'll let you know next December. Happy New Year to you and yours.

August 16, 1975

Our First Dove Season

When I was at Ft. Riley Kansas in 1964, I had the opportunity to do a lot of hunting. One of the most sought after game birds was the dove, a bird I never had the chance to hunt in Ohio because it was protected. There were millions of doves in Kansas, and it seemed that most of them flew by many of the sunflower plots we had on post. Needless to say, I fired a lot of shells that year and ate a lot of doves.

In 1975, I was excited to learn that Ohio would have its first dove hunting season. Of course, there was a lot of controversy, but the season took place. 1976 was another good dove year as the sport gained in popularity. In 1977, a Federal Judge in Toledo ruled that the Ohio Division of Wildlife didn't have the right to establish a dove season, and hunting was stopped.

What followed for years was a comedy of errors. The politicians got involved, and the political maneuvering began. There were some legislators who saw that a dove season was based on sound wildlife management. Others spent their time counting the votes they would lose when they tried to get reelected. In one case, the House passed a bill, but the President of the Senate refused to bring legislation to the floor for a vote. It wasn't until 1994 that the House finally passed a bill that authorized Wildlife to set another season. Two years later, anti-hunters got an issue on the ballot to stop the dove season, but hunters prevailed.

Dove hunting had a stormy beginning in Ohio. Now that it's established, many hunters enjoy the sport. Although the bird is small, it provides excellent table fare. Bag limits and season dates are based on sound management practices. Declaring the dove a game bird was a sound move. Anti-hunters didn't agree then, and I'm sure they don't agree now. After reviewing the dove statistics, the season made sense to me. It was definitely an interesting issue.

Outdoors with Forda Birds

Anti Groups Attack First Dove Season

Right before I took off for a little fishing a couple of weeks ago, the Division of Wildlife announced that there would be a dove season in certain areas for Ohio. It wasn't too long after the announcement that reports began filtering in concerning a movement by members of the legislature to stop this new season. Both Senate and House bills were introduced during the last week of the General Assembly. As soon as the Assembly recessed, the anti-hunting forces came out of the woodwork and began a concentrated effort to stop the September season.

The anti-hunting groups began to sound off and with, what appears to be large financial backing, started their campaign to turn more citizens not only against dove hunting, but against all forms of hunting. Some of you may have seen the ¼ page ad that appeared in some of the larger metropolitan newspapers. It was, in this writer's opinion, one of the most charged pieces of writing I've ever come across. It stated very little defense for their position but simply took shot after shot at the sport of hunting. They stated that they believed it was wrong for a seven man Wildlife Council to establish game laws without approval of the legislature. Of course, this is a valid debatable point. But, what takes the cake is their loaded series of statements that follow and really show what they are trying to do. In plain words, the anti-groups that are supporting the elimination of the dove season could really care less about one, any, or all doves. What they are trying to do is to use this case as a club to push for their ultimate goal...the elimination of all hunting. Why else would they leave the arguments concerning the pro's and con's of dove hunting and say, "It is clear to us, that as usual, the hunter is not as hungry as he is bloodthirsty for the thrill of the kill." That's hogwash, and the fact that people who think like that can muster so much support to sell their message flat scares me.

What's going to happen to the dove season? Right now it's anyone's guess. There will probably be a short session of the Assembly this September and something may be done at that time. Also, there is a possibility that an injunction might be obtained to stop the season before it gets off the ground. I really don't know.

One thing I do know is that hunters and the pro-hunting groups had better get busy and make themselves heard. The anit-groups are suggesting that everyone write to the Governor and tell him how they feel. I suggest the same thing. But, before you decide to send any note to Columbus, think the issue through trying as much as possible to ignore the emotion that is bound to enter into your decision. Consider the following: 250,000,000 doves are produced annually in the U.S. Ohio recorded a 35 per cent increase over 1974. They are a major game species in over 30 other states. Approximately 75 per cent of the preseason population dies each year from natural causes. Life expectancy is just one plus years. 75 percent of the 6,000,000 doves in Ohio will die whether they are hunted or not. This is a loss of 4,500,000 doves that could be used by Ohio hunters under controlled conditions for food and recreation.

It really doesn't do much good to apply statistics to this type of decision especially when a true anti-hunter is approached. Facts and figures are fine if they help support your argument, but if they don't apply, the anti's ignore them.

Regardless, the anti-hunting groups in this country are strong and growing stronger every time an issue like this comes into light. This is August 16. Have you waterfowl hunters wondered why the federal wildlife guidelines haven't been released yet? They are being held up because of interference by the anti-hunting groups that almost prevented a waterfowl season from opening last year. Don't let anyone ever try to tell you that anit-hunting is not a serious threat in this country. It is, and we have to sound off and stop it.

I usually have the chance to voice a lot of opinions when I write this little piece, and with that freedom I can honestly say that we wouldn't have the game we have today if we did not have wildlife management and managed hunting. Millions of dollars are spent each year by the sportsmen to buy land for wildlife purposes and keep it out of the hands of the developers. Most of all, anti-hunting groups fail to spend one thin dime for game propagation, establishment of wildlife preserves, or any other related outdoor activity.

The goal of the anit-hunting groups is to stop all forms of hunting. And…they're going to do it even if they have to kill every animal in the United States. Doesn't make much sense, does it?

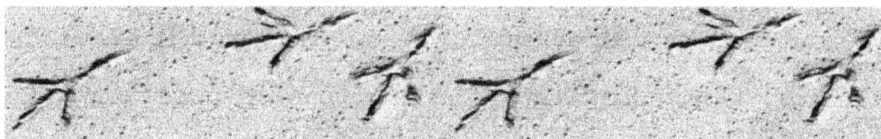

May 8, 1976

McMurray's Striper

Putting striped bass in the lake was a grand experiment. The federal hatcheries developed a successful breeding protocol, and striper fry and fingerlings became available for Ohio stocking. Stripers were put into two Ohio lakes that I know of, Lake St. Marys and West Branch Reservoir. After a number of years when they became legal to keep, an occasional large fish showed up which guaranteed someone would hold a state record.

Although there were few, Lake St. Marys produced the most big fish while West Branch, for many years, never had a striper caught on hook and line that I know of. That's ironic because Ohio's record striped bass eventually came from West Branch, a 37 pound, 10 ounce monster taken in 1993.

Regardless of weight, I'll always consider Mike McMurray's 29 ¾ pound striped bass a record fish. If I remember the account, Mike fought the fish and after tiring it out, tried to land it by hand. At that point the line broke. While the exhausted fish floated near the shore, McMurray went into the water, cradled the fish in his arms, and carried it up the bank. It's interesting to note that the fish was caught off the East Bank, and McMurray had to scramble down and up the rocks to land the fish. That feat alone makes the fish a record in my books. Of course, a 35 pound fish was taken off the West Bank that same year, I believe, but the circumstances weren't as exciting as McMurray's. I'll always contend that McMurray holds our lake record. If nothing more, I'll give it to him on style points. He earned his fish.

The severe cold weather in the beginning of 1977 caused the lake to freeze almost to the bottom in the shallower areas. When the ice finally left, official reports showed that the carcasses of at least 100 potential record-breaking stripers were found along the north shore of the lake from the Sailboat Club to the golf course. For all practical purposes, the winter of 1977 ended an exciting fishing chapter at Lake St. Marys. The Feds dropped their stocking program, and stripers were never stocked again at Lake St. Marys.

100

Outdoors with Forda Bird

A New State Record

I'm just about ready to give up on the striped bass predictions. It seems that every time I get on the horn and start making fun of these fish, or lack of fish, another big one finds the net. And, this time it looks as if a new state record has been established.

Friday afternoon about 2:30, Mike McMurray of Wapakoneta hooked into the fish off the East Bank. He was fishing for catfish and using cutbait. After an obvious battle, he landed a striper that, when officially recognized, will break the existing record by more than 4 pounds. McMurray's striper measured 39 inches and tipped the scales at 29 ¾ pounds. The current record is held by Carolyn Felss of Cincinnati, Ohio with her 25 ½ pounder caught last year. Felss' fish was caught on a blood bait called Catfish Charlie.

Yes, the striper story in this area is getting more confusing every day. First of all, with the number of fish stocked, there just shouldn't be many, if any, caught. This statement is based on their stocking that has been done in the state. Stripers have been stocked in one other lake in Ohio, West Branch. The program began about the same time as ours, and to date I don't believe any large fish have ever been reported. As a matter of act, in recent conversations with outdoor writers from that area, it is questionable whether or not any of the West Branch fish have been taken on hook and line.

Another thing that makes the St. Marys striper a unique fish is the phenomenal growth rate. These large fish that are being taken today have come from either the 1967 or 1968 stocking. It's amazing that they've been able to adapt themselves to conditions in Lake St. Marys and live this long. Granted, they have an over abundant supply of food, but let's face it, our lake just isn't striper territory. What's even more amazing is that even though fishermen continue to catch these fish I continue to keep saying that there aren't any more in the lake and none bigger will ever be caught.

With that last thought in mind, I think I'll just stop and say no more. Heck, if I predict this new record might soon be broken it probably will never happen. So, I'll go out on a limb and say that this new record will stand for a long time. And, if the pattern continues to be the same, it might be interesting and worth while to give the striper fishing a go. I have a lousy track record

101

when it comes to predictions, and if I say the striper fishing is finished, someone will surely prove me wrong. Here's hoping one of you keeps my record from being smashed.

From time to time I get static from people who say I should be talking about fish I catch. Well, I seldom do for many reasons. One of the main reasons I keep the "kills" out of the paper is that getting the fish or game is not my main enjoyment in going outdoors. Now, don't get me wrong. The day I catch a record striper or a ten pound bass I'll let everybody and their brother know about it. But, unless it has some purpose, I doubt if I'll ever change my mind on the subject.

Now, this should be confusing because I will tell you that I and a fellow outdoor writer did make a pretty good catch of crappies last Saturday northeast of Fremont in Green Creek. We caught enough to feed fifteen people and had more than enough left over to stick in the freezer. The fish were running large and one stringer of 40 fish weighed 35 pounds.

The main reason for this report is that there are many good fishing areas in the state. All one has to do is keep the eyes and ears and give them a try. Also, a little luck can help make any fishing trip a success.

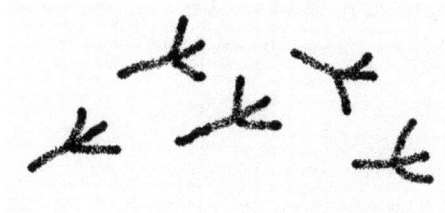

February 12, October 8, October 22, 1977

Dove Season Gets the Axe,
Leghold Trap on the Ballot

I believe that 1977 was a pivotal year for the Ohio sportsman. Until that time there appeared to be very little sportsman unity. Hunters concentrated on hunting and were ignoring the increasing influence the anti-hunting groups were having on their sports. In February, after two dove seasons, a Federal Judge in Toledo ruled that the Division of Wildlife did not have the authority to establish a dove season. Regardless of the judge's justification for the ruling, the anti-hunting groups touted it as a success for their movement, and probably rightly so.

The next issue that came to the forefront was one that would ban the leghold trap. Those in favor of the ban declared that this type of trap was inhumane and should be outlawed. Taking the debate aside, the movement was another challenge by the anti-groups in their quest to eliminate not only trapping but the hunting sports as well.

The following three columns follow Issue 2 and are significant in that, for the first time, outdoor sportsmen finally realized that their sports were on the chopping block. If Issue 2 passed, other attacks would soon follow, and with the phenomenal amount of funding that the anti-groups were generating, it was only a matter of time before not only trapping but hunting would only be found as a footnote in some history book.

Issue 2 was soundly defeated by the voters. As a result, trappers and hunters recognized the power they had if they worked together, and from that moment on, species specific organizations began to sprout up across the country. The very fact that outdoor sportsmen recognized the power of numbers probably saved hunting, trapping, and even fishing from becoming a history lesson. One of the oldest sportsman's groups, Ducks Unlimited, became the model for other organizations. Suddenly, saving our pheasants and their habitat became a priority and Pheasants Forever was formed. The Ruffed Grouse Society, Quail Unlimited, Whitetails Unlimited, The Wild Turkey

103

Federation, The Rocky Mountain Elk Foundation and others suddenly appeared lending credence to the fact that sportsmen were serious about their sports and intended to fight for their existence.

There is no doubt that 1977 signaled the birth of an attitude, an attitude that reflected the sportsman's solidarity, something that was sorely missing.

Outdoors with Forda Birds

Ohio Dove Get the Axe
Banning the Leghold Trap:
A Dangerous Precedent

Last week, the Count of Appeals in Lucas County overruled a previous lower court decision and delivered an opinion that stops the hunting of dove in Ohio. I haven't read the decision, but from what I understand, it was well written and not the typical loaded ruling that one might expect in such a controversial issue.

Whatever the case, the next step is up to the Ohio Department of Natural Resources and the Division of Wildlife. They have to study the ruling and determine if and when the matter should be taken to the Ohio Supreme Court. I would assume that our highest court will eventually have the matter dropped in their laps, but as it stands today, there will be no dove hunting this fall in the state.

It appears that the leghold trap issue will be on the November ballot. I'm not about to debate the issue, but I think that people who are opposed to the leghold trap, including some hunters, should look very closely at the issue and the obvious effects that will follow if it becomes law.

First of all, Ohio has evidently been chosen by the large-anti-hunting organizations as a test state. They played an important role in the dove issue, but even more, have made a strong effort to promote the ban of the leghold trap.

I know that many people carried petitions with the only idea that leghold traps were cruel, and they wanted them outlawed. Unfortunately, this is not the real issue, and no matter how sincere, those who support this ban are being used by groups whose ultimate goal is to stop all forms of hunting and, yes, even fishing.

No one likes to be told they are off base, and even though it may look like it, that is not my intention. However, I can give you something to think about, and you can judge for yourself. If this leghold trap issue gets on the ballot and should pass, the following things would happen. First of all, the traps would be outlawed and the people who worked hard to accomplish this goal would be happy. At the same time, however, this passage would establish a precedent creating the first step in issuing something now called the "Animal Bill of Rights." And, if this "Bill" should ever become law, all hunting and fishing would be stopped, and with it would stop the monies that these sports generate in order to be self-sustaining.

Let's face the facts, if wildlife monies are stopped, you might as well say goodbye to all the fish and wildlife as well as the habitat they enjoy, That would make this state a mighty sterile place to live in, and only the land developers would ever cherish the thought. So, what it boils down to is this. If you are against the use of the leghold trap, that is acceptable as far as I'm concerned. But remember, in supporting this bit of legislation, you are also saying that all hunting and fishing should be stopped, the Division of Wildlife should be abolished, and all wildlife management and protection should come to a halt.

Division of Wildlife is Responsible for ALL Wildlife

The Ohio Division of Wildlife is responsible for all of Ohio's wild creatures and not just the sport species. Consequently, since their only revenues come from hunting and fishing licenses and federal taxes on firearms and other related equipment, the elimination of these two sports would also finish this agency.

So what? Well, I wonder just who or what group would pick up the tab to insure that when we take our kids outdoors, they have a chance to see the creatures we have enjoyed for so many years. True, this big change won't happen overnight, but it wouldn't surprise me, if trends continue, that many of us will be around to see it take place.

Outdoors with Forda Birds

Issue 2: What is it?

An amendment to the Ohio Constitution will be placed on the ballot for all voters to consider this Election Day. It's known as the "Leghold Trap" Issue, or better yet, as Issue 2. Proponents of this amendment contend that the leghold trap is "inhumane" and that it should be outlawed. But, the method they chose to get their point across spells more problems for the people of this state than meets the eye. This proposed amendment would not only stop the leghold trap but would also put an end to all forms of trapping. Now, the proponents of this issue might say that I'm reading more into the proposal than is really there. Well, all of us have a right to interpret, and I'm sure that there are bound to be some judges somewhere who would see the short comings as I and many others see them.

The only way to get to the basics of the problem is to tear it apart, piece by piece. Following is the language of the proposed amendment.

Section 1. No person shall use in any manner in the trapping of wild birds or wild quadrupeds any leghold trap in this state.

First of all, it is illegal in Ohio to trap wild birds by any method. But even more than that, the proposal states that leghold traps cannot be used to trap any wild quadrupeds. This, I assume, includes not only the valuable fur bearers but also other wild four legged critters such as rats and mice. If this is the case, the disastrous results are obvious.

Section 1 (cont.) No person shall use any trapping device in a manner which will cause continued, prolonged suffering to a wild bird or wild quadruped in this state.

The proponents of this issue state that the amendment only applies to the leghold trap. However, this statement seems to me to include any and all forms of traps including live traps. For example, placing a wild animal in captivity in a live trap will cause suffering simply because the animal doesn't want to be there. I bet it wouldn't be long before even the box trap would be determined as an "inhumane" trapping device.

Section 2. Each separate violation of this amendment constitutes a crime.

I question the appropriateness of placing this type of statement in the State Constitution. The Constitution is to contain principles of government and

106

methods to protect the rights of the people. It is general in nature to insure the flexibility needed to even function at all. Consequently, something as specific as Section 2 would tie the hands of those who are sworn to uphold the Ohio Constitution and this is not proper.

Section 2 (Cont.) In addition, any person may bring a civil action in any Common Pleas Court for an injunction to stop violations of this amendment. Such person may recover the costs of the action and reasonable attorneys' fees.

Now, I don't know how you read this statement, but the way it appears to me is that if this issue passes and I have to catch a mouse who is eating me out of house and home, anyone who catches me doing this deed can bring charges. Not only would I have to answer to these charges, but I would have to foot the bill while the person bringing the action could recover the court costs and attorneys fees. There has to be a legal term for getting put behind the eight-ball. And, there would be a lot of people in that condition if any Tom, Dick, or Harry decided to press the issue. Heck, I wouldn't object too strongly if I could get involved in a court action without having to worry about paying the bills if I lost.

I am no lawyer. I don't know the law. But, I am a voter and just reading this proposed Issue 2 frankly scares the devil out of me. I've just scratched the surface of this "leghold" controversy. The adverse effects on our game management, the health hazard, and many more aspects should be considered. What it all boils down to right now is that the Issue will be on the ballot, and it must be defeated. What is even more disconcerting is the fact that Issue 2 even made it as far as it did. Heaven help us, a heck of a lot of people in this state just weren't thinking straight.

Outdoors with Forda Birds

More on Issue 2

On Election Day, the voters of Ohio will be faced with a decision concerning the proposed banning of the leghold trap. With any issue, there are undoubtedly two sides, and both of these are being presented to the public through the various communication media. But, unlike other issues we've seen over the years, Issue 2 has turned into a highly emotional one and this is too bad.

I am against Issue 2 as you can well see. It is not because I'm a trapper. I have no personal interest in trapping and wouldn't know how to set a good trap if I wanted to. I don't have close friends in the fur business and surely don't make a dollar from the practice.

The reasons I am opposed to this issue, though, are, at least to me, valid, and these I'd like to share with you. In my last column on Issue 2, I tried to interpret what I saw as the shortcomings of the amendment as written. It is generally accepted by the legal profession that this proposed amendment has no place as Article 19 of our Constitution. I respect this opinion. Also, being involved with the English language, I can see that the issue is not only wordy, but vague enough to create problems for law makers and judges across the state. Those two points alone are enough to turn me against the issue.

But even more than that, I feel that this issue is a direct attack on the practice of wildlife management. Species of animals are controlled to maintain a healthy balance. The statement made by the proponents of this issue say that nature will control the balance. In theory, this is correct provided that there is no interference by man—none at all. And, this type of environment is impossible to achieve because no matter where man lives, he leaves his impact.

What effect would a ban on leghold traps create? First of all, a surplus of wild animals brings about the possibility of increased disease problems such as mange, distemper, rabies, tularemia, and others. Many of these are highly contagious and communicable to livestock, poultry and domestic pets. And, the leghold trap is, at this date, the most humane, selective trap available. The alternative is a trap known as the Conibear which is known as the "instant kill" type.

Proponents tell me that this theory is a bunch of hogwash. I wouldn't agree or disagree unless I've seen it proved. In Missouri, a few years ago, I spent a month in the sticks on a field problem. One of the biggest concerns we had were the wild animals in the area. The habitat was ideal and the human population was small. Consequently, the animal population was high and so was the presence of rabies. Another area of the world that proved the point was Vietnam. The jungles were ideal wildlife habitat, and any soldier who spent time in the bush knew that you just didn't mess with the animal population, wild or domestic. As a matter of fact, having been a combat medic, I know of a number of people who had to take the rabies series because of a scratch or bite from an animal. In plain words, it would be hard to convince me that over population wouldn't cause disease problems. Locally, we have a rabies problem to some degree. Last year, for example, it was reported that approximately 50 rabid raccoon were destroyed in this area alone.

Like it or not, wildlife management is necessary if we want wildlife. Man's impact dictates this practice. If this weren't the case, flies shouldn't be killed, mosquitoes shouldn't be eliminated, gardens shouldn't be weeded, and any number of other examples.

Yes, these are opinions, but I think they show some thought. Now, what I want the proponents of Issue 2 to present are alternative plans. Tell me how you intend to control our wildlife resources. Tell me the benefits you intend to give mankind. Make your point and I'll be happy to use this space to present it. I've received letters, and I guarantee that if I use one, I'll use them all.

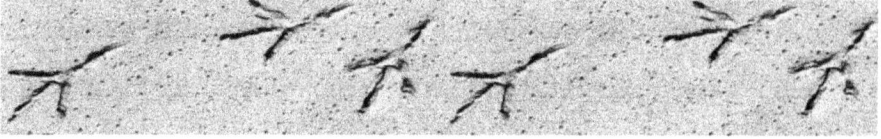

December 31, 1977

Remember the Cold?

There were many notable events that happened in 1977, but the one that will be remembered is the bitterly cold January and February we had to suffer through. January 1977 was the coldest month known in Ohio. The average temperature for the month was 11 degrees which was 17 degrees below normal. The temperature never got above freezing all of January, and if my memory is decent, there was one stretch of 12 days when the temperature never got above zero.

Many businesses, factories, and government buildings had to adjust their schedules because of shortages of natural gas. The whole state was hit by this cold spell, and even Cincinnati had record temperatures of 25 below zero. The weather moderated very little during the first half of February, and temperatures of 20 below zero were recorded.

Fortunately, by the end of February temperatures in the 60 degree range started to show up, and what the history books will show is that most people were resilient enough to handle the brutal temperatures Mother Nature decided to hand us. Fish and wildlife, however, had a rough time surviving. Many sportsmen took it upon themselves to provide extra feed for the wild critters. Backyard bird feeders gained in popularity during this period. One of the biggest loses in the area was a large number of giant striped bass. Since the water in Lake St. Marys was relatively low, the ice in many parts froze almost to the bottom. These big fish couldn't handle the conditions, and for all practical purposes, the striper fishery, although limited, came to an end because of this enormous winter fish kill.

A number of other important events took place in 1977, but the record cold all across Ohio will be the one that gets passed down from generation to generation.

Outdoors with Forda Birds

Goodbye 1977

This is it…the end of another year. Some people, of course, will mark 1977 as the best year ever while others might wish it had never arrived. Whatever the case, "77" is now history and for the outdoorsman, there were more than enough significant happenings that took place.

The big story of the year, however, would have to be the record winter we suffered through during the first months. The energy shortage caused more problems than we like to talk about, and the long stretches of bitterly cold weather raised havoc with all of nature. The results of last winter will probably never be totally realized, but it is evident that many of the state's lakes and ponds suffered heavy fish kill. Also, many species of animals suffered abnormal cuts in their population. All in all, the now infamous "Winter of 77" is one that most of us hope we never see again.

The second big story of the year had to be the Leghold Trap Issue. This issue, of course, made it on the November ballot, and the voters defeated it by a two to one margin. This issue was hard fought, highly emotional, and in many cases could be considered one of the most important decisions that Ohio voters have faced in many years. The outcome, in my opinion, was the right one.

Another important event in Ohio was the elimination of the dove season. This was decided as a result of a ruling handed down by the Court of Appeals in Lucas County. It was important not in that it was good, it was important that it created an awareness in many Ohio sportsmen that the anti-hunting movement was real, active, and here to stay.

There were a number of other stories and happenings that rate a mention in 1977. The lake, of course, had very little water in it. This in turn created problems for boaters as well as fishermen. It appears that the water problem might be on the way out, however. Recent rains and snow have brought the old puddle back to a decent level. Now, all we need are regular spring rains to sustain it through the hot months. Also, the stopping of the dredges didn't do the lake any good. The stoppage was caused by the Corps of Engineers, but this problem should be eliminated with the lake being put under the jurisdiction of one Engineer Office instead of two.

Strange animals appeared this year. One of them, north of here, had a taste for sheep and eliminated hundreds of the animals. No one seems to know what happened to the creature. While I was in Michigan, a retired Michigan State Police Lieutenant spotted Big Foot tracks near my vacation retreat. These tracks and other sightings caused a coffee shop in that area to put "Big Foot Specials" on their menus. You could also buy "Big Foot" guns. And, if you wanted to look for the monster, a "Bigfoot Guide Service" was available. So, it looks like 1977 might have been called the year of the monster.

Other stories for 1977 include a gun season for deer in Auglaize County. This is the first time in many years that deer were allowed to be hunted with firearms in the area. The decision was based on a solid deer population around this neck of the woods. Many local fishermen enjoyed the fabulous walleye fishing on Lake Erie. Even I came home with a mess of fish. A fellow from Toledo caught two potential record fish in the Chagrin River. Both of them have since been disqualified since it was discovered that they were caught in Michigan.

There were countless other little happenings this year. Some were good, some bad, but all of them added up to one of the most interesting years we've had in a long time. So, good-bye 1977! Hello 1978! And, a Happy New Year to all!

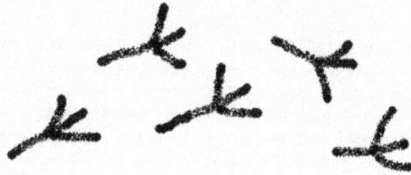

Three Feet of Snow; 70 mph Winds

On Wednesday evening, January 25, 1978, I was at the Winchester Public Shooting Center indulging myself with a few rounds of skeet. I was enjoying the unseasonably warm weather and remember that I wore a windbreaker over a light sport shirt. There was a light mist developing, but shooting conditions were excellent. I paid little attention to the weather warnings that called for extreme blizzard conditions in a matter of hours.

By early morning of January 26, the winter weather did arrive and many of those who doubted the severity suddenly found themselves just trying to survive the elements. Wind and snow hit with a vengeance followed by the extreme cold. Sustained winds of 50 to 70 miles an hour with gusts close to 100 miles per hour blew copious amounts of the white stuff into enormous drifts. Cars were quickly covered, and in some cases even houses totally succumbed to the three feet of blowing snow. In one particular instance, a semi tractor and trailer were completely buried, and the driver wasn't discovered for a week.

I can recall trying to walk to my father's house that was just three blocks away. I had to seek refuge behind buildings because the wind and blowing snow kept freezing my eyes shut. It was a record storm. The barometric pressure measured 28.28, the lowest ever recorded. For lack of a better description, we were caught in the middle of an inland hurricane.

The storm lasted into Saturday, and everything was closed. It took five days before people could move around safely, and even then, it would be weeks before conditions got back to normal. Snow was removed and dumped on the tennis courts behind Memorial High School. There was still some snow on the site on May 15, according to my notes.

No one knew how bad the storm was until it was over. The column I wrote said little about the weather's severity. What it did was suggest ways people could keep warm. Looking back, I could have come up with better advice than I did. What it does reflect, however, is that people were in shock over the immensity of the storm. The fluff piece I wrote didn't add to my reader's concerns; I don't think it did much to inspire them, either. You be the judge.

Outdoors with Forda Birds

Coping with the Blizzard

Someday I might have grandkids who will want to know what I was doing during the winters of "77" and "78". Well, at this stage of the game I'd be hard pressed to give them an answer. One thing for sure, I was making myself comfortable and trying to do things that kept my mind off the miserable weather.

You know, if you want to get cold and develop a good case of "cabin fever", the best thing you can do is sit in front of a window and watch the wind blow piles of snow against your door. Another good method for feeling miserable is to listen to news broadcasts. Even though these fellows provide a valuable service, just listening to what they have to offer can really cool you down.

Myself, I'm a realist. Yes, I looked out the window and saw the mess we have, and I started getting cold. So, I stopped looking out the window and just forgot about it. Heck, just what was I going to do about it? Not a thing. And on top of that, when I started thinking about other residents across the state, especially those without power, I really started counting my blessings and warmed considerably.

What to do when you're snowbound? Well, I don't know about you, but I directed my thinking to warmer days. I did some writing, but not as much as I could have. I outlined a couple of magazine articles, and got a good start on a feature about Lake St. Marys fishing that is supposed to be on the editor's desk by February 10. I worked on a gun stock for a couple of hours, and spent some time in my darkroom. True, I didn't accomplish that much, but I kept busy, at least busy enough to keep my mind off of the weather. Oh yes, I also got the opportunity to play a lot more with my little girl which warms you up quicker than anything else.

So, one can survive when nature gets a little wild. It's a state of mind, and believe it or not, man has quite a bit of control over that. So, before I get ready to walk this column to the paper, I think I'll wrestle with my kid for a bit, play a fast game of Jack Straws, and then go out and brave the elements.

I had the opportunity to talk to the Loramie Lake Improvement Association a couple of days ago, and really enjoyed myself. My talk was centered on the recreational potential we have with Loramie, Lake St. Marys, and the Miami-Erie Canal that joins them both. After the talk, a question was brought up as to what I thought of forming some form of organization that would push to develop the whole area recreationally. I hope my answer came out that the idea had a lot of merit. It would seem that the various Lake Associations, Chambers of Commerce, and other interested groups could form a power base that it takes to let our legislature know that this area is important to all of the people in Ohio.

Whatever, the idea has been presented and I'd like to hear some comments. And, once more, thanks to the LLIA for having me as their guest.

As soon as I can get myself dug out, I have to start thinking about working on some fishing tackle. This is an annual job for me, but I enjoy doing it. Heck, once I get into it, I'm sure my mind is going to wander back to last summer when I caught a 10 pound brown trout off of a pier in Frankfort, Michigan, or maybe back to the great day I had walleye fishing on Lake Erie. Or maybe, I'll just sit back and think about those four big bass I took one evening just off of Birch Ridge.

I'm warming up already, and that means it's time to end this column for another week.

September 30, 1978

No More Quail

In the early 19th Century, there were few bobwhite quail in Ohio because the habitat wasn't appropriate to sustain them. A quail is not a forest bird. As trees were cleared and more farm land developed, quail began to appear in good numbers. By the 1860s, the quail population was not only solid but wide spread. Farming practices provided edge cover for the birds, and they could move to food and water with protection from predators.

Quail are not particularly hardy birds, and it's estimated that up to 80% of them succumb to weather, disease, and predation within a year. Nature does provide for this weakness by giving quail the ability to breed prolifically. Unfortunately, being able to produce a large number of offspring isn't necessarily enough. Along with habitat loss, weather has been the quail's major nemesis.

Severe winters during the early part of the 20th Century played havoc with the quail population. Then farming practices began to change and the weedy fencerows many of us remember and hunted in became history. The winter of 1977 and 1978 was the coldest ever recorded. When spring finally arrived, it was estimated that 90% of the quail had been destroyed. Game managers weren't overly concerned because of the quail's ability to populate in good habitat. Within a few years, the quail population should be back to normal. These same game management specialists became more than totally concerned when the great blizzard of 1978 hit. Concern grew to panic, and rightly so. Across the state, the remaining quail couldn't survive the brutal winter conditions. In some southern counties, a few birds survived. North of Interstate 70, for all practical purposes, these small game birds were completely eliminated.

Quail survival is directly proportional to good habitat, and good habitat depends on decisions made by man. At this time, farmers can't justify taking any farmland out of production. First, land is expensive. Second, with grain bringing high prices, it isn't good business to leave buffer strips for game birds.

Upland game birds need food, water, and protective cover to get to these resources. A fall-plowed, clean-farmed field provides none of that. Now, throw in an extreme winter, and it's no wonder there are no quail. Since we're on the extreme northern range of these birds, it takes ideal habitat and mild winters to insure a viable quail population. Since we seldom have either one, don't expect a huntable quail population very soon in this part of the state. Come to think of it, since upland game doesn't seem to be a priority in Ohio anymore, I wouldn't look for it at all.

Outdoors with Forda Birds

No Quail Season for 1978

After the winter of 1976-77, hunters were concerned about the quail population in Ohio. And, when last fall rolled around and the upland game season opened, their concerns turned out to be a reality. There just weren't any quail to be found. Granted, a few survivors were still making a go in certain parts of Ohio, but for all practical purposes, the Ohio quail population was in trouble.

However, even though the quail population was at its lowest in years, conservationists weren't too concerned since a high annual mortality rate is expected. Some figures show that as much as 80 percent of the game bird's population die each year because of natural causes. Consequently, Mother Nature provides the quail with the ability to produce a large number of young to take care of the losses that take place each year from weather, disease, and predators.

Something unexpected happened in 1977, however, that really clobbered what was left of the quail. In case you've forgotten, it was the winter of 1977-78 which dumped record snows on the area and made life for our wildlife next to impossible. All animals were hard hit, and the quail was no exception. What remained of the already low population was practically decimated, and figures show the population today is approximately 90 percent below the last 17 years average.

With this in mind, Dale Haney, Chief of the Division of Wildlife recently announced a program to get the quail population back in order. Haney said, "We will follow sound biological principles which will include a habitat management program, restocking programs, and closure of the 1978 quail season in Ohio.

According to the Division of Wildlife, the management program will include advice to land managers designed to improve habitat. Farmers will be asked to leave a row or two of soybeans or unharvested corn for quail already present. Delayed mowing of fields and other areas during the nesting periods of June and July will also increase nesting success.

The second phase of the program will include the restocking of quail in areas that were hardest hit. This will begin this fall with the trapping of wild birds in Ohio. These birds will be kept in holding pens through the winter and the eggs that are hatched next spring will be held for one full year. These birds will be released into the wild prior to the 1979 breeding season.

The last part of the program is one that hunters should pay particular attention to. Haney said, "The third portion of the program is based on the present population of quail. The 1978 hunting season will not be opened this year. This action does not include commercial shooting preserves or dog training grounds which remain open by statute."

So, it looks as if the Ohio quail hunter will have to go some place else if he wants to bag a quail or two, and rightly he should. You know, people kick game management procedures much of the time, and the anti-hunters are the best at this. However, even though this decision to stop the quail season for this year is a disappointment for many hunters, I don't think you would find very many that would gripe. The results of the past two winters were obvious, and the hunter knows that only game management will give him any kind of a chance that he will have game to hunt in the future.

Quail management for Ohio is underway, and hunters, land owners, and all concerned should make an effort to do what they can to help it along. It would also help if Mother Nature got off her "high horse" and did the same thing. The weather prognosticators are predicting a mean winter for 1978-79. The quail just can't afford a mean winter, and man could do without one, too.

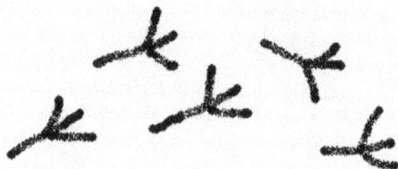

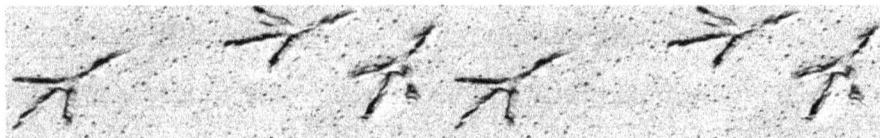

November 4, 1978

The Pheasant Pledge

I never got that involved with politics, and I never ran for elected office. I helped my friend, Ed Stepleton, with a campaign or two, but that was primarily for entertainment. As far as running for office, Ed once told me that if I wasn't running with the intention to seek a higher position, I was wasting my time. I believe I could have landed a city council seat and maybe even wound up in the mayor's office, but neither job interested me. I found it more enjoyable to sit off to the side and let others duke it out.

The 1978 gubernatorial election struck my fancy, however. Jim Rhodes was trying for his fourth term in office, and I thought he had been there long enough. Besides, he promised a cash bonus for teachers, and that never happened. Consequently, I couldn't find it in my heart to vote for a guy who owed me $500.

Rhodes was challenged by Dick Celeste who I believe was a former Lieutenant Governor. I didn't know much about the guy, but right before the election, I received a campaign letter in which Celeste pledged all sorts of initiatives related to the outdoors. In a nut shell, he promised more of everything. Fish, deer, turkeys, waterfowl, pheasants, you name it. Celeste was going to develop programs to improve the numbers of all these species.

Celeste lost the election and Jim Rhodes got to serve his fourth term. In 1982, Celeste ran again and was successful since Rhodes had to sit out for at least one term. Rhodes tried to take out Celeste in 1986, but the incumbent prevailed.

I liked Dick Celeste. Although a politician, I think he was sincere about his outdoor platform. I know he wanted the outdoor writers to sign on. As a matter of fact, he made it a point to invite us in small groups to the Governor's Mansion to discuss his ideas. It was a nice house, by the way, with a big back yard.

A couple of years later at a press outing on Lake Erie, a writer friend and I were jammed into a marina to ride out a storm. To avoid the crush of people,

119

we snuck into a back room with our coffee, sat down, and relaxed. When Celeste arrived at the marina and his security saw how packed the place was, they ushered him through the crowd and pushed him into the room where we were sitting without checking it out first. He stayed there for 30 minutes or so, and my friend and I had another nice talk with the governor. I'd already spent a couple of hours with the guy at his house, so it's not that we didn't know each other. There was no bull, no posturing, we just chewed the fat. Of course, his security was miffed when they found us in the room. We thought it was funny; they didn't. Celeste sent them back out, and we stayed there until the storm subsided. Yes, I liked Celeste. He never got the pheasants back, but that's okay. He gave it a shot. Besides, he didn't owe me a dime like the other guy did.

Outdoors with Forda Birds

What Celeste Has To Say

Tuesday is Election Day and because of this I recently received a letter from Lt. Gov. Dick Celeste who is running for governor. The purpose of his letter was obvious. He was making a point to let the outdoor communicators as well as other selected sportsmen know what his stand was on Ohio's outdoor future. Since I haven't seen any mention of this, what he has to say is worth sharing even though it is general in nature.

First of all, if elected, Celeste pledges that the Ohio Department of Natural Resources will "maintain an active and progressive program for the promotion of good conservation practices throughout the state." He also states that he will, "direct that greater emphasis be placed on the propagation of game fish for release in our lakes and streams." He promises to, "promote and closely monitor Ohio's growing deer herd in accordance with good game management procedures." He wants to, "continue the programs to reestablish and broaden the range of the wild turkey...protect and further develop our marshes and wetlands to encourage and expand our waterfowl population...encourage and promote the reestablishment of adequate food supplies and habitat on both public and private lands for the improvement of our small game population...and embark upon a special program to effectively restore the ring-necked pheasant to its rightful place as the state's No. 1 game bird."

Celeste concludes his statement by saying, "the Department of Natural Resources will work in close cooperation and harmony with the numerous conservation clubs, sportsmen organizations, and with the Wildlife Council in order to carry out these mandates. I want to see Ohio rank in the forefront of our fifty states in the development and preservation of these precious resources."

No one can fault what Celeste has to say. To me, what he wants to do has a great deal of merit. Unfortunately, actually getting these things accomplished is easier said than done. First of all, funding is and always has been a problem for our natural resources program. When one starts talking about habitat development, for example, the only practical method to accomplish this would probably be to subsidize property owners to develop portions of their land into good habitat areas. With property costs what they are today, this cost in itself would be prohibitive. Reestablishing the pheasant also is a good idea, but unless habitat is restored, this project would never work.

Whatever the case, I can find no fault with what Celeste wants to do with our natural resources if elected governor. And, if he is elected, I would be more than willing to do my part to help these things take place. However, that's what Election Day is all about, and when the people make their choice, I'll know what actions I should be taking.

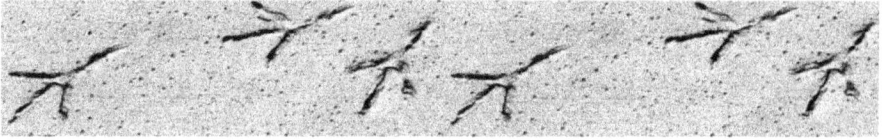

December 30, 1978

Count On More Pheasants

It seemed ironic that in 1978 everyone was talking about restoring pheasants in Ohio. Celeste pledged that he would restore pheasants as Ohio's number one game bird if elected governor. He wasn't. Then in December, Carl Mosley, Wildlife Chief announced a plan to bring pheasants back to Ohio. What caused this sudden interest? First, the devastating winters of 1977 and 1978 had reduced the existing population of ring necks some 96 percent. Also, ever changing farming practices made it almost impossible for these colorful game birds to survive. "Sloppy" farming provided good pheasant habitat, clean farming didn't.

If I remember correctly, it was Earl Butz, Secretary of Agriculture, who started promoting greater grain production to fill foreign grain needs. Farmers began tilling all available land. They cut hayfields earlier, killed weeds, mowed road ditches, and plowed under remaining grain stubble as soon as crops were removed. Soon fences were removed. Yes, it was great to see all of the grain fields being planted and the resulting crops. After harvest, however, all of these farm lands looked like deserts.

Basically, Mosley's plan called for mowing to be suspended throughout the nesting season. If farmers cooperated, birds would be stocked on this protected property. The one doubt I had was that farmers wouldn't be willing to cooperate. For all practical purposes they didn't, and the restoration project died a slow death, as did the remaining pheasant population. Again, it's ironic that farming practices created a massive Ohio pheasant population, and farming practices, likewise, destroyed it.

Biologists finally figured it out, too. Weather didn't destroy the pheasants, hunting had little impact, and predators that ate the young or destroyed the eggs weren't the major culprits. It was a question of habitat. Appropriate food sources, all-season cover, and adequate water would restore the pheasants. In 1978, with clean and efficient farming practices, it seemed unlikely that these conditions would ever appear again.

I think the Division of Wildlife gave up on the pheasants at that time. They still stocked a few each fall, and hunters flocked to the release sites in hopes of bagging a bird. Ohio pheasant stocking, I believe, was nothing more than an attempt to get some good press and appease hunters because stocking birds had nothing to do with population restoration.

In 1982, a group called Pheasants Forever was formed with the philosophy that restoration of habitat would ultimately restore the pheasant. Today, the group has many chapters working to achieve this goal. Federal programs, such as CRP, were initiated later in the 1980s to improve habitat.

In the 1950s, a lot of land north of here was in the Soil Bank program. I remember hunting these fields. In many cases, they were so thick it was difficult to walk through them. They held birds. I should have made the habitat connection back then.

Regardless, Mosley was right on with his plan. Unfortunately, it was doomed before it started.

Outdoors with Forda Birds

New Pheasant
Restoration Program Announced

A few days ago, Carl Mosley, Chief of the Ohio Division of Wildlife, announced a program to restore pheasants in Ohio. According to Mosley, "Three critical components of wildlife habitat have been lost or seriously reduced in the intensively farmed regions of Ohio. Work will start with the agricultural community and government agencies to develop long-term solutions. Short-term projects are being designed to provide immediate results this coming summer and will mesh with the long-term effort."

The three problems this new program will attempt to solve is the lack of nesting cover that is permitted to stay uncut through mid-August, woody cover, and winter food supplies. As these areas are dealt with, pheasants will be stocked within their historic range and heavier stocking can be expected where the critical habitat needs are best met.

According to the program, pheasants will be released following certain criteria. Eight 10-week-old pheasants will be stocked for each three-acre unit of undisturbed hayfield on each 80 acres of farmland. Ten-acre units of undisturbed hayfields available for a two year period will be stocked with 10 adult pheasants. In addition, day-old chicks will be supplied for groups such as 4-H and FFA, and others with suitable facilities where three acre tracts of undisturbed hayfield can be provided.

At this stage of the game, it appears that the program has merit. However, before any judgment can be made, a great deal more information should, and, I'm sure, will be announced in the near future. Right now, I'm trying to see some of the problems that might appear. The first one that really hits me is what degree of cooperation will the Division of Wildlife get from the property owners when they present them their program. As Mr. Mosley said, many areas of Ohio are intensively farmed. I wonder if the farmers who are trying to make a buck will want to change any of the land practices they now take part in. One of the components needed for pheasants, according to this program, is a winter food supply. This area is a prime example of what has happened to the winter food. Fall plowing leaves nothing for the wildlife during the hard months of winter and that lack of food must take its toll of animals each year.

But, I'm not about to tear down a program that hasn't had a chance to work. I would love to have a pheasant population around here again. The last bird I bagged in Auglaize County was in 1959 and that makes for a long dry spell. However, I do feel that no matter what type of program the state comes up with, success can only be equated to the amount of mutual cooperation that can be generated. If the area farmers, sportsman clubs, and interested outdoorsmen get behind this program, the chances of success greatly increase. And, if the Division of Wildlife makes an effort to talk with instead of talk at the people, success will be even closer.

I'm sure I'll be receiving more information about this program in the next couple of months and will probably talk with Mr. Mosley in some depth about the subject in early April. When I find out exactly what is going on, I'll be able to report to you in greater depth. And, if you want to investigate the program on your own or are interested in participating, you can contact someone who is in the know at the following address: Ohio Department of Natural Resources, Division of Wildlife, Attn: Habitat Program, Fountain Square, Columbus, OH 43224.

Gosh, wouldn't it be great to see a pheasant or two next year when we hit the field on opening day. Let's hope that this program takes hold. By golly, it sounds like a start.

May 19, 1979

Who Trusts Politicians?

I'm not politically savvy. As a matter of fact, I'm probably politically naive. I should have paid more attention in my high school American History and American Government classes. Hell, for a long time, I thought we lived in a democracy until Barry Kemp once reminded me we lived in a republic. I guess I should have paid more attention to the words of the Pledge of Allegiance instead of just memorizing them…. "and to the republic for which it stands."

Anyhow, for those who don't know, and the way I understand it, a republic is a form of government that doesn't have a king. In our case we elect a president. In a republic, individuals don't have a great impact on government, but those we elect to represent us do. The way I see it, that makes us a representative democracy. Now, that's where it gets sticky. We elect people to represent us, and somewhere during this process we either lose confidence or distrust them. In case you haven't heard, a significant percentage of the people think their elected officials are crooks, or at the very least, shady. How in the world can a person be elected to a state or national office without owing somebody? And, if you owe, you're expected to pay. How can any worthy piece of legislation be passed using a system that is inefficient by its design?

Making deals, being influenced by lobbyists, selling out, and pork barreling are all accepted practices, I guess. It's a question of power bases and committee appointments, democrats and republicans, liberals and conservatives. I think the American people get frustrated because it seems that very few politicians look at the merits of the legislation they propose or pass. There always seems to be some underlying juggling act that gets in the way.

In 1978, I had little confidence in our state legislators. I've probably refined that attitude over the years, but when I start to trust a politician, I always remember one of my dad's many one-liners. "Son, if you put a republican, a democrat, and an s.o.b. in a barrel and roll them down a hill, there's always going to be an s.o.b. on top."

Anyhow, the following column was generated by my attitude at the time.

125

Outdoors with Forda Birds

Outdoors and Politics

I received a comment this week from a person who didn't appreciate me calling legislators, "bumbling idiots." I apologize for making that statement even though they appear to take on this identity from time to time. In fact, I have come to the conclusion that when a legislator appears to be a "ding bat" on the surface, underneath he is really an intelligent, concerned, thoughtful, streetwise, shifty, pawn of the politics he serves.

Who am I to say such things about our elected officials? Just a citizen, I guess. Politics aren't my cup of tea and the inner workings of this system are a mystery to me. All I do know is that my gut feeling tells me that I and the other average Joe citizens are not getting the service they deserve.

Take the fuel issue for a moment. Congress started dealing with an emergency rationing system and in the end, it went down the tubes. I won't go so far as to say whether this was good or bad. What I object to is the method and reasoning that the final conclusion was reached. Of course, I can't read the minds of the guys who did the voting, but from the reports I've had and from what I've seen and heard on the evening news, decisions were made not on the basis of the legislation, but rather on how the political wheels happened to be turning at the time. Legislators supposedly voted against this proposal because they feared losing some votes. Others voted against the issue because they had ties with the oil companies. Others voted against the issue because it was initiated by the opposite party. And, I'm sure that others voted the way they did because of reasons that had some other political overtones. I wonder why these gentlemen can't look at a problem and vote on a proposed solution entirely on the merits of what is presented. If the opposite party initiates a decent piece of legislation, why shouldn't it be supported if it would be good for the country?

Assuming that we will be having more fuel problems in the future, our law makers will have their hands full. These problems are serious and there isn't time for our elected officials to play their silly political games. I've read the American people have little confidence in their government and this is sad. What frustrates me more is that even though I try to give people the benefit of the doubt, I am rapidly losing confidence in our elected officials, too.

I received a press release from the Wildlife Legislative Fund this week and, right or wrong, the information it contained really floored me. It dealt with the proposed dove hunting in Ohio. Now, I'm not saying one word whether dove hunting is proper or not in Ohio. I have my opinions and some of you have yours. What burns me up is that our state legislators are involving this issue in their political ball game and aren't even bothering to look at the issue itself.

Last year, Senator Ocasek supposedly said that the dove bill might pass and as President of the Senate simply refused to allow further proceedings. What ever happened to due process? How can these legislators do their job if they can't register a vote? The article went on to explain how Ocasek established his Rules Committee for this year. He evidently loaded it with his cronies which in turn gives him one great deal of power. The President of the Senate is the man who can do other people favors. He can make them look good politically. He assigns committee chairmanships. In plain words, he stacks the deck in his favor.

Outdoor related? Sure it is! Our legislators have a great deal to say about what the outdoors will be like in the future. What gravels my craw is that I don't think our legislators consider anything unless it is approached through their political values, and by golly, that's one serious sin in my book.

July 14, 1979

Changes: Big and Small

I've discovered a couple of things over the years. First, the older you get, the more time is compressed. The fact that I've been writing this column for 40 years seems like nothing. The 25 years before when I was growing up seemed like an eternity. Second, what I think is significant would probably mean little to anyone else. Now, let me try to explain.

When I was a youngster, one of the most exciting events of the day would be a fishing trip to the lake. My stomping ground was the Miami-Erie Canal behind my house. That's where I played, that's where I fished. Since I wasn't mobile, going anywhere was a big event.

My dad tied our cane poles to the door handles of a 1937 Plymouth, and we headed for Haeseker's Bait Shop located along the East Bank. It was a run-down place that hung out over the swamp old timers used to call the "dismals." Anyhow, old man Haeseker made small talk with my dad; we bought a couple of dozen minnows and headed out to wherever the fish were supposed to be biting. Sometimes we caught a mess, sometimes not. It made little difference. For some odd reason, that hole-in-the-wall tackle store was a place that sticks in my memory, and I really don't know why.

30 years later, old man Haeseker's son built a new shop where the "Outdoorsman" is now located. When I heard they had sold their business, it was a bit emotional. I wasn't particularly close to either Lou or Nina. I did have a pretty good relationship with them, and over the years got used to Lou complaining a lot about this and that. I remember one person saying that if someone dumped a truckload of gold bricks in Lou's front yard, he'd complain that they didn't stack them.

Regardless, not having a Haesaker on the East Bank seemed like an end to an era. It helped remind me that times change and things come to an end. It reminded me that I was growing older, and that my life was heading somewhere and picking up speed.

Since I started writing this column in 1969, I've lost my grandparents, my parents, a sister, a mother-in-law, and a couple of brother-in-laws. At the same time, I had three kids and now have a couple of grand kids. It's no wonder that time seems to fly.

As far as the significance of Haeseker's Bait Shop, there really isn't any. The ownership has changed a couple of times, and the business is probably better run than when Lou and Nina had it. I guess another lesson I learned is that life went on without Lou and Nina, and life will go on someday without Forda Birds. In the grand scheme of things, none of us are significant. It's how we affect other people that's significant.

Outdoors with Forda Birds

Haeseker's Bait Shop under New Ownership

The other day I happened to stop in at Lou and Nina's to chew the fat and see if there was any type of fishing report. But, neither Lou nor Nina was there. Instead, I was greeted by one of the new owners, Roger Simonson. Of course, I had known that this change was about to take place, but it was a shock to walk through that door and not see Lou or his wife behind the counter.

To say that these people are an institution in these parts is an understatement. I can remember from almost day one when I used to go into the old bait shop Lou's dad had along the east bank and buy minnows. And, even before I was fishing alone, I can remember going into that old place with my mom and dad to pick up bait for a little fishing off the old east wall.

To make a long story short, the Haesekers were known by just about every local fisherman and thousands of others who happened to make their way to the lake. To me, they provided a bit of local color that made it enjoyable to just walk through the door, Along with the service they provided, these people will be missed by many, and I know that I can be counted as one of them.

However, as trite as it may sound, times change, and it appears that "Lou and Nina's," now called "Bass Ackwards", is getting off to a good start. According to Roger, the business will be open year-round and will cater not only to the fishermen but to the hunter as well. If this is the case, this business could be a great addition to the area sportsmen. There are many possible fall and winter activities at the lake, but it seems that when the summer season ends, everyone closes shop. There are times when I have wanted to give the ice fishing a shot but found it almost impossible to buy bait. Also when the duck hunting season opened, I have wanted a place close by to check in with other hunters to see how they have been doing. It appears that "Bass Ackwards" just might be that place.

So, out with the old and in with the new. I wish the best of luck to the Haesekers and hope that everything goes their way. I also wish good fortune to the Simonson's and hope that their business prospers. What they plan to do with their shop sounds interesting. I hope that all of their plans work out and we continue to have a first-class business at this end of the lake. So, drop in and introduce yourself and let these people know that we local lake rats aren't half bad people.

As I write this column, I have a little girl sitting next to me who suddenly has the desire to write something like her dad. After trying to come up with reasons why this shouldn't be done, I just gave up and told her that if she wanted to give it a shot, the rest of this column was hers. I guess what bothers me the most is that what she puts down might say more than what I can come up with. Regardless, let me present this column's first guess writer.

Fishing at the Lake
By Terri Andreoni (Age 7)

This summer my dad and I went to Michigan for two whole weeks. I use a rod and a reel and we catch a lot of fish. So far this year, I caught over twenty fish. The other night we had a fish fry and I ate some of my fish. They were good. Sometimes when we go fishing we put them back in the water. But I still have fun fishing and playing in and out of the water at the lake here and in Michigan.

July 28, 1979

Are Hunters Insecure?

I learned about the sport of hunting from my dad. I knew what type of territory might hold a rabbit or a pheasant. I also knew that a lot of walking was involved. Waterfowl was another story. It took a bit more sophistication to be a successful waterfowl hunter. First, there was the art of concealment. Next came the strategies of decoying. Calling was included in the instructions, but neither of us was ever good at it.

Most of all, however, I learned that you had to play by the rules. Hunting on private property was a privilege not a right. One never hunted without permission. All game laws had to be followed to the letter, according to my dad. That's why the laws were there.

How strict was my father? I don't know how he operated in the field before I came along, but when we hunted together, there was no one who followed the rules closer. One particular instance still sits with me because I remember being very upset about his rules interpretation. We were hunting at Prairie Creek starting off from what was then Malone's Landing. We had rowed to the back waters, set out a few duck decoys, and saw nothing until the last minutes of the day. A small bunch of Canada geese were heading our way and there was a chance we would get a shot. This was quite unusual. At that time, geese were scarce. I had never shot at one before, but that wasn't unexpected since I was only 12. The geese continued to come closer, finally set their wings, and started to flutter down. My heart was pumping as I rubbed the hammer of the single-barrel shotgun I was carrying. I waited for him to tell me to shoot as I watched the geese settle. Instead, he stood up and said, "Quitting time."

Of course, when the geese saw him stand, they flared, and that was it. I was almost in tears when I asked him why he stood up. He simply pointed to his watch. Not one minute late. That's the way he played the game. Had I been alone, I would have shot. I know it. Today, I probably wouldn't. I guess that's the way a responsible hunter is supposed to act.

Unfortunately, the majority of hunters didn't learn to play by my dad's rules. Most would, at the very least, bend them a little to fit the purpose. Some would ignore all game laws and do whatever it took to fill their game bag. Those are what were referred to as the slob hunters.

For the sport of hunting to continue, the hunter image has to be without blemish. Those against hunting use the slob hunter as the sport's poster child. It's not fair because the majority of hunters are decent folk. Unfortunately, when people see or hear about the slob hunter, they apply the definition to all. The only way to stop that injustice is to eliminate the slob hunter and for the rest of us to be squeaky clean. It might not be right, but it's real.

Outdoors with Forda Birds

The Hunter Image

In "Reports from Washington," a paper put out by the NRA Institute for Legislative Action, I came across a little filler that dealt with the images of hunters. Now, some of us have read some of the comments made by the anti-hunting faction, and if they were to describe the hunter they would state, "Hunters are insecure people who engage in a sick activity with no useful purpose that has no place in society today."

To answer these charges, the National Shooting Sports Foundation had some research done that showed that these "problems" rank well down the list of bad points. What the research did show, however, is that the major concern about hunters today is that they are improperly prepared to practice the sport of hunting and have a lack of concern for the rights of fellow sportsmen.

These findings I tend to believe. If I had to categorize a large percentage of hunters, I would describe them as being inadequate shots, lacking in knowledge about the sport of hunting, and practically unfit to carry a firearm in a field with another hunter anywhere in the area. They ignore safety precautions because they really aren't aware that any should be taken. It doesn't take a genius to see these characters when they hit the field. And, if you do happen to spot a few this fall, my suggestion to you would be to head for the hills.

Yes, it is true that lack of knowledge is a problem that many "hunters" have today. But, even a bigger problem is that lack of concern not only for their fellow hunters but the property owners as well. All of us have come across hunters who we would love to kick square in the seat. They shoot over your

132

decoys, they shoot in your direction, they walk onto the area you're hunting without permission, and generally make a pain in the nose of themselves.

What hurts the sport of hunting even more is the fact that these same characters have even less respect for the property owner. I have watched hunters cut fences so that their dogs could get through. I have watched hunters tromp down unharvested crops. I have seen hunters hunt without permission then raise the devil with the property owner when he asked them to leave. Two years ago, I went to the farm I usually hunt waterfowl and found a duck blind built along a standing corn field made from unpicked corn. And, these characters made a sizeable hole right in the middle of the field. A couple of other hunters dug a pit right in the middle of the field the same dimensions as a grave. When they finished hunting, they put a piece of plywood over it and covered the wood with dirt. Unfortunately, they never returned to hunt and the farmer discovered the pit with his tractor. To say the least, this property owner was upset, and I know there is no hunting allowed on his property.

The one good thing about the problems I've been mentioning is that they can be corrected. And, any sportsman who has done these things in the past or will do them in the future should start thinking what impact his actions are making on the sport. The anti-hunting faction in this country is strong, and they are looking for instances that would make the sport look bad. On top of that, property owners are getting sick and tired of hunters walking all over their property making general nuisances of themselves. From what I've seen and heard, it amazes me that there are any property owners around willing to let people hunt on their land.

What this all boils down to is that hunters everywhere should start examining their actions when they hit the field and make sure they act like the sportsmen they are supposed to be. If they do, we may be able to enjoy the sport of hunting for the rest of our lives. If hunters fail to make a change for the better, we might be around to see the day when hunting becomes something we just read about in a history book.

1st *Hunter Safety Course*

When the Hunter Safety Course became an Ohio requirement to purchase a hunting license, I wasn't concerned. After all, it didn't apply to me. If anything, I leaned toward the position that making safety training mandatory was a good idea.

Since I wanted to find out about the course, I took my daughter, who was just shy of eight-years old, to the Moulton Gun Club, and we both took the three nights of training. It wasn't that difficult. I think my daughter only missed five questions, but she was pretty smart. No, daddy didn't help her. She already knew about hunting, fishing, the outdoors, and such. As a matter of fact, although I might have violated some child-labor laws, I had her reloading shotgun shells when she was six.

Regardless, about this same time, the number of Ohio hunters began to decline. Whether or not the Hunter Safety Program had an impact on hunter numbers is debatable. However, something caused a decrease in youngsters entering the sport. I'm sure for some, spending three evenings of training seemed like a lot of hoop-jumping to get a hunting license. Also, if parents weren't actively involved in the sport, who would take the kids? Besides, many hunters thought it was not only their responsibility but their right to determine when their kid hunted and what they needed to know.

It took awhile, almost 30 years, but a compromise was finally reached. A program called "Families Afield" was initiated built around basic core values. Safety first, always. Hunting instills traditional values, connectivity with nature, and healthy lifestyles. Parents, not politics, should decide an appropriate hunting age for their children. When introducing youth to hunting, earlier is better. Youth experience hunting with an adult mentor then attend a hunter education class.

As a result of "Families Afield," Ohio now has an apprentice hunting license. Youngsters can experience hunting with adult supervision without hunter training. They have three years to determine if they enjoy the sport enough to take the required hunter safety program.

Many states are adopting similar measures in an attempt to increase hunter numbers, at least that's the hope of the National Shooting Sports Foundation and other organizations. How successful the initiative becomes is still to be determined. I guess this is one of the movements I get to watch for the next few years.

Outdoors with Forda Birds

1979 Hunting Licenses on Sale

One of the sure signs that the summer season is almost over is when we find ourselves heading out to purchase our new hunting license. Well, that time is here again, and you need a new license as of today.

There aren't too many changes in the license regulations for this year, but what changes there are happen to be quite significant. The cost of an annual resident license is $7 plus a 75 cent writing fee. All hunters must have a license regardless of age. Residents over age 65 or older may purchase a permanent hunting license at any agency selling resident hunting licenses. Previously, permanent hunting licenses could only be obtained at the county court house.

Something new this year is the trapping permit. This permit is required in addition to a hunting license for all those who plan on giving trapping a shot. The cost of the permit is $5 plus a 75 cent writing fee.

The biggest change for this year applies to all new hunters. According to Senate Bill 419, the hunting license applicant must meet certain requirements before being issued a license. Applicants must present their hunting license bought in any previous year from any state or Canadian province, or they must present evidence of having completed a hunter safety program or present a notarized statement that says the applicant is 21 years old or older and is not a first time hunter.

This new law might sound a bit complicated and possibly seem unnecessary to many. However, I think it has its place in the hunter's scheme of things. First of all, hunters are under the gun by anti-factions who are constantly looking for bad apples in the field. They are looking for the hunter who doesn't know the laws or has little, if any, knowledge about conservation or game management. These people shouldn't be in the field, and this law will help keep them in check. Consequently, if you are a first time hunter, you have a responsibility to the sport and to the rest of the hunters around you to know what you're doing before you make your first showing.

Hunters who have had previous experience should not consider themselves something special. Just because you have had a previous license doesn't make you an expert. In many cases, some "experienced" hunters still don't know anything about the outdoors. So, new hunters shouldn't feel self-conscious if they find themselves in a hunter safety conservation course. And, those of us who have been hunting for years might also benefit from this type of training. It seems to me that anything we might learn about hunting will do nothing but improve the sport, improve our image to the public, and possibly give us a bit more enjoyment when the season rolls around.

Hunter Safety Course Scheduled for Auglaize County

A free hunter safety course will be offered this coming week at the Moulton Gun Club just east of Moulton. The course will run on three consecutive evenings beginning September 4 and ending on September 6. The sessions begin at 5:30pm and run until 8:30pm. Each session of any course must be attended and upon successful completion of a course, a hunter safety certificate will be awarded. The courses are open to all interested persons and no advanced registration is required.

So, if you have a youngster who is ready to hunt this year, make an effort to get him or her to these meetings. And dads, it might be a nice gesture if you took the course with your son or daughter.

Annual Duck Blind Drawing

Across the state, blind drawings for those seeking preferred sites will take place next Saturday. The drawing for blinds at Lake St. Marys will be held at the Mercer County Wildlife Area headquarters located south of Celina on SR 703. The drawing will begin at 10a.m. following registration. Hunters must register for all drawings in person and must have a new hunting license and a current waterfowl stamp.

From past experience, let me suggest that you get to the area well before the 10:00 drawing. This event usually draws close to 1000 hunters, and it's usually good to get there on time to make sure that you don't miss out on your chance and at the same time help the procedure move along.

September 29, 1979

The Future of Lake St. Marys

Lake St. Marys is a shallow body of water that sits in western Ohio's farm country. It was designed as a feeder lake for the Miami-Erie Canal system and provided a north-flow water source. When the canal system finally collapsed as a result of the 1913 flood, what little transportation there was ceased to exist. In reality, the canal ceased to be part of Ohio's transportation infrastructure as soon as the railroad came into existence.

Oil was discovered along the shore and under the waters of the lake, and during the late 1800's, working oil derricks dotted the entire area. With the discovery of high-yield wells in Oklahoma and other states, pumping "black gold" stopped although there were still a few wells producing into the 20th Century.

In the early 1900's, the lake was designated by the state as a recreational area to be enjoyed by the public. Prior to that, it was used as a cash cow by market hunters and market fishermen. After this dedication, the lake truly became a multiple use recreational area. Waterfowl hunters enjoyed fabulous hunting, and sport fishermen took advantage of superb fishing. The lake even supported an amusement park for vacationers including a large roller coaster that, from reports, gave a fabulous view of the lake.

Over the years, however, especially during the depression, this development stopped. Funding was at the mercy of the legislature, and monies for continued development dried up quickly.

The lake had its problems, though. Silt poured into the shallow basin in quantities large enough to quickly destroy it. As a result, a dredging program was initiated. At best, this program was never more than a stop-gap measure. It was postponing the inevitable. More drastic measures had to be adopted to save what was once known as the largest man-made lake in the world.

When the Director of the Ohio Department of Natural Resources came to the area to talk about the lake, I was excited. Promises were made at that meeting, and I forecasted great things happening at Lake St. Marys over the next five years. Unfortunately, that was 30 years ago, and I'm still waiting.

Outdoors with Forda Birds

"Something will be done."

I attended the joint meeting of the Celina and St. Marys Chambers of Commerce the other night and listened to Bob Teater, Director of the Ohio Department of Natural Resources, state that Grand Lake St. Marys had nowhere to go but up. Having known the director since he took his present position, I probably appreciated what he had to say a bit more than some in attendance. The main reason I say that is based on his track record over the years. I think Dr. Teater is a highly qualified individual who doesn't waste his time making idle promises. He just doesn't seem the type of guy to cater to any special interest group and surely isn't about to sacrifice his opinions for the sake of appeasing people. In plain words, when the man says something will be done here at this lake, I take him at his word.

I would caution the Lake Development Corporation, however, to recognize completely their role. What they have accomplished so far is tremendous. They have unified the entire area in pursuit of a common goal. At the same time, this organization has created an immediate power base that will make it a group to be listened to in Columbus.

This power is a two edged sword. If it is used in such a manner that forceful direction and persuasion can be leveled at appropriate times to keep the lake development process moving, the LDC will do more good than can be imagined. On the other hand, if this group suddenly becomes one who starts banging on doors and making a nuisance of themselves, they will soon find all Columbus doors locked to them.

From what I have seen of the LDC and from what I know of the group, I have a tendency to think they will act prudently in their dealings with the ODNR. This will spell success for them. They will have a more than important place in the development of this area, but should keep in mind that decisions to work on Lake St. Marys were not totally based on the influence of the LDC. The current philosophy of the ODNR is to focus attention on outdoor recreation in Ohio. It is their idea that Ohioan's should spend time in their home state and that facilities should be made available for them.

Dr. Teater related in his comments that there is just so much water area in Ohio to develop into recreational areas. Building lakes the size of Lake St. Marys is prohibitive simply because of the cost. This means that Lake St. Marys is in store for a face-lifting because it is here. The fact that is exists in 1979 almost guarantees that something will and must be done.

Whatever the case, I have nothing but positive feelings about the future of the lake. The main concern can be spelled out in terms of dollars and cents. This money will come from the legislature, and it is obvious that the LDC will have something to say about these future plans. As far as the future of the lake is concerned, it is sooner than we think. I guess I should go out on the limb and predict that within five years, we should be seeing some big changes in our "puddle." These changes will take place courtesy of the LDC and the ODNR working together toward a common goal. Both groups will get what they want. The ODNR will acquire a large quality outdoor recreation site, and the LDC will eliminate the problems that give many of us a bad feeling about this body of water we call our own.

October 13, 1979

The First 10 Years

It seemed to me that the 10th anniversary of this column would be an appropriate place to end this first volume. Initially, I planned to do just one book, but when I started picking and choosing what I thought were significant entries, I discovered that I managed to say quite a bit over the years. At least, that's what I thought. Okay, so events had a lot to do with it, but regardless, I quickly saw that it would take more than one volume to cover forty years, over 2000 columns, and over 1.5 million words not counting the other stuff I managed to pawn off.

Think about it. That's a stack of paper 20 inches high. If you put the pages end to end, they would stretch out more than a mile. I'm still the highest paid outdoor writer the *Leader* has ever had. I still have the longest running outdoor column, and my predictions still have problems although I think I'm getting better since I don't make that many any more.

Another reason I stopped here is that I wanted time to catch my breath. There was a lot going on during the first ten years. The winters of 1977 and 1978 were enough to take the wind out of anyone's sails. The high water year of 1972 still stands out as a freak of nature. I think it was referred to as a once-in-a-hundred year event. Don't forget the energy crisis of 1974. We were supposed to be out of oil five years ago in 2004. And finally, the biggest story for 1979 was a new oil crunch. As I said then, everyone is looking to see gasoline go over $1.00 a gallon. What a way to end a book.

So, I concluded a decade of columns with the following piece of fluff that said very little, and that's being nice. On the other hand, it did put all of those words in perspective. Now, it's on to the next ten years. I hope they were as interesting as the first ten. I'll have to read them again to refresh my memory.

Outdoors with Forda Birds

It's Been 10 Years

I've never been the one to remember dates, but my wife soon broke me of that after I forgot our first wedding anniversary. Since that time, I have been conscious of all kinds of dates, and October 13 has some significance. It applies to this column, too.

On October 14, 1969, the first column I wrote about the outdoors appeared in *The Evening Leader*. That's ten years ago! What a milestone for me and maybe a milestone for you. During that time, I have accomplished many goals and received more recognition than I can deal with. For example, I have the longest running outdoor column ever to appear in the *Leader* since I can remember. I am the highest paid outdoor writer the *Leader* ever had, as far as I know. And most of all, I have made more wrong predictions concerning the outdoors than any outdoor writer the *Leader* ever employed.

So, you're not impressed. Did you ever stop to think just how much writing I have actually done for *The Evening Leader* these last ten years? Let me tell you, a bunch, a whole bunch! Just to prove the point, I sat down last night and came up with the following statistics that should give you an idea of jut how much toil and trouble have gone into this column since it began. If you took all of the copy I put together and put it in a pile, it would reach up a staggering distance of 4 ¼ inches. That's compacted, of course. If you put every sheet of 11" typing paper end to end that has carried Forda Birds on it, it would reach almost around the world....would you believe across the state....how about 980 feet. Actually, I could cover my bathroom walls four times with these columns, including the floor.

What the heck, who really cares how much material I've written for this column over the years. One thing I do know for sure, I have enjoyed doing it. I hope you have enjoyed reading all, some, or part of it, and I appreciate the fact that the *Leader* has gone along with me for all of these years. My wish is that I can continue doing this little bit each week for a long time to come.

The bowhunting season for deer opened yesterday, and I will be waiting to hear any results. Bowhunting is gaining popularity in this neck of the woods. This is being caused by the fact that we have a great deal more deer in the area, and also because many sportsmen of today are looking for the challenge.

Going after a deer with a bow is indeed a challenge. A hunter is fortunate to get a good shot during the season, and even this is more of an exception rather than the rule. Can you imagine what type of hunter it would take to spend hours in a stand waiting for just one split second, that perfect shot? I know that I don't have the patience to try it myself, but I just might give it a go someday.

The opening day of the duck and goose season also came up yesterday. October 12 is one of the earliest opening dates I can recall, and hunters may have a few problems because of it. The hunters who spend their time on the lake should have decent luck since we do have a good supply of local birds. However, hunters on the lake are always bothered with other problems such as heavy competition and the inevitable cloudbusting.

Field hunters will have problems since the farmers are having difficulty harvesting crops. The weather has been a pain for them and bumper crops of beans and corn are starting to look like they never will be taken in. But, I have seen the road hunters out in good numbers so they must not be letting the late harvest bother them.

Whatever the case, these two seasons are in and this puts the 1979 hunting season off to a good start. I'm glad it's here.

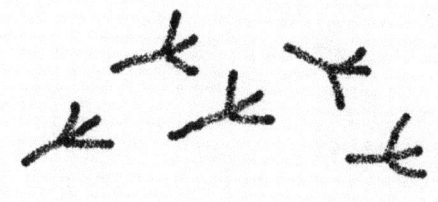

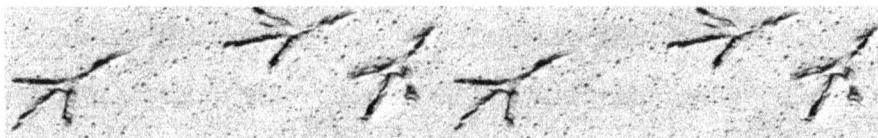

1976: A Bicentennial Special

The nation's Bicentennial Celebration took place on July 4, 1976, the 200th anniversary of the adoption of the Declaration of Independence. Of course, the celebration really began a year earlier, but the major whoopla, at least according to the major television networks, started on July 3 and ended on July 4th with a day's festivities that ended with a slam bam fireworks display in Washington. Other major cities also spent a ton of money firing rockets into the air.

I remember seeing the collection of tall-masted sailing ships in New York Harbor. I heard that a group of people celebrated the Boston Tea Party by throwing boxes labeled Gulf Oil and Exxon into the harbor. People still weren't too happy with the oil companies. The Queen of England showed up, for what reason I don't know. It was a grand time, and a good reminder that although we suffered a potential constitutional crisis with Nixon's shenanigans, the country survived and was prospering.

Regardless, I wanted to do something monumental for this special event. After a certain amount of thought, I decided to write a story about a local piece of history that had an effect on the development of the country, albeit a minor one. I once referred to the Miami-Erie Canal as the, "8th Wonder of the World." If it was that important, it deserved a shout. How to approach the topic was the next consideration. I finally decided to step out of the box and write a piece of fiction that depicted the hard work and sacrifice that thousands of people provided to dig the "Big Ditch." I figured it represented all of those seeking a better life who helped make this country what it is today. Did I accomplish my goal? It seems to me that I did. At least, I felt that way back in 1976. Anyhow, for the record, I thought this short story deserved a spot in the first volume of, *Going Wild with Forda Birds.*

A Canal Story

By John Andreoni

Editor's note: Sean McQuae was not a real person in the sense that he lived and breathed, but he represents thousands of people that were involved in the making of the Miami-Erie Canal and seeking the "American Dream." While he did not live in the sense of a real person, his spirit was alive during those canal building days as immigrants dug the "big ditch".

Sean McQuae was just one of the thousands of Irish immigrants to come to the New World in the 1840's and like most, he liked what he saw. At least, he knew it was better than what he had left. True, the Atlantic crossing was a trial but was bearable especially since the alternative would have been a long, possibly permanent stay in an Irish jail.

All tenant farmers on the Emerald Isle were having problems and Sean had dealt with them longer than most. But, between an unscrupulous landlord and ever growing taxes, he had finally reached his boiling point. It seemed like only yesterday that he had broken into the large manor house and helped himself to some loose silver. The screams and shouts when he was discovered, however, still rang in his ears. And, the gnawing fear he felt as he ran, continuing to run until he reached Queenstown and boarded a ship for New York still formed a knot in his stomach. But he had survived, and now he stood in a new land where things could be different.

As he followed one of the crowds that constantly flowed through the harbor area, he listened to the excited jabber of people like himself moving quickly yet not really knowing where they were going. They would, of course, eventually have to stop, and when they did, it was inevitable that an Irish community would spring up. The Irish were gregarious people and they loved being together, but Sean McQuae had had enough of Ireland and Irishmen. And besides, how soon would it be before word filtered back to Queenstown, County Cork, the authorities and his irate landlord that he was living in an Irish community in New York City? No, he had to move on.

"Hey, Irish Johnnies," a voice sounded above all the rest. "A chance of a lifetime is yours. Triple wages, board, a roof over your head, and all the whiskey you can drink. There's work on the canals and we want you."

144

Sean was drawn to the booming voice like some of the others and as he listened to the promises of riches, whiskey, and an (occasional) mention of work, he had the sudden feeling that the Maker was finally answering one of his prayers. "This America is indeed grand," he thought to himself. "I haven't been here more than a few hours and already I'm provided for. I have to eat. I can work any two men into the ground, and a jug of whiskey will handle the rest."

Sean worked his way closer and soon found himself in front of a table facing a well dressed, portly gentleman with a smile that ran ear to ear. "Well, Johnny, are you ready to build canals?"

"The name is Sean. Sean McQuae. Where do I sign?"

He placed his name on a list, stepped back, and surveyed that grinning, stone face. Sean had a talent for judging character and his initial impressions left him cold. That face would surely shatter if it smiled any harder and the eyes were too narrow for an honest man. But, his feelings vanished as the man said, "Here's $3 and a flask of the best, my lad. Go in that building, get something to eat, and relax after your long journey. We'll be leaving in a little while."

As he opened the door, he was greeted by happy voices and the strong smell of food simmering over a huge open hearth. It was a good smell and as his plate was piled high with beef, beans, and bread he suddenly realized how hungry he really was. Toward the end of the voyage, the food aboard ship had spoiled or at least sported a solid covering of high green mold. And now, he was eating better and more than he had ever thought possible. He sat down in a corner, took a long draught from his newly acquired jug, and began to satisfy his empty stomach. "What a country," he thought. "Less than a day in America and already I'm a wealthy man. Food fit for a king, money in my pocket, and enough whiskey to celebrate my good fortune." Sean emptied his plate, devoured a second helping, took one more pull from his jug and fell into a deep sleep.

Sean and 20 other young Irishmen traveled up the Hudson to Albany then boarded a canal boat and began their journey along the Erie Canal. The entire trip was a pleasure and their new employer made sure that there was a constant supply of food and drink. With little to do but bask in the sun and relax, it didn't take long before Sean lost all of the fears and anxieties that had heretofore made his life miserable. And, from the laughing and joking that rang all over the boat, it appeared that everyone was feeling content.

The canal boat soon reached Buffalo and immediately the new arrivals were hustled aboard a small sailing vessel and herded across Lake Erie to Toledo. At Toledo, their employer again assembled them at a local tavern and still plying them with food and drink introduced them to a new face. "Gentlemen, this is Mr. O'Neil. Stay close to him because he'll be taking you to Fort Wayne. Then, you'll be in the canal business."

The grin was still there and Sean could not remember an instant when it had shrunk one bit. Then, the man stood and in the same tone of voice he had used in New York said, "Well, Johnnies, it's back to New York for me. Maybe we'll meet again some day." And with that, he turned and was gone.

"Quite a fellow," a companion said. "What was his name?"

Sean thought for a moment and said, "You know, I don't believe I ever heard it mentioned. It's no concern though, my friend. Forget about it and let's build us a canal."

The trip to Ft. Wayne from Toledo was slow but the excitement made the time pass. There was new country to see, new people to talk to, and the evening stops with the revelry that took place still gave the men a feeling that their adventure was nothing more than a game. They walked the entire distance at an almost leisurely pace generally following the Maumee River, occasionally breaking off to go across country. O'Neil led the party and also seemed to take the trip as a lark. But, in a few short days the journey was over and Sean McQuae along with 20 other Irishmen were in canal country.

Well boys, I'm back to Toledo in a day or so to bring another batch of you fellows." And, O'Neil continued, "It's been a pleasure sharing your company."

"Mr. O'Neil, Sir, begging your pardon. Where do we go from here?" said McQuae.

"Oh yes, I almost forgot. Boys, this here's a ditch, called a canal. All you have to do is follow it and I guarantee you'll be finding work. This whole stretch is bossed by a man named Russel. He's fair, pays top dollar." And, he added with a barely noticeable grin, "You'll earn it too."

The small group of Irishmen discussed their situation and after weighing the pro's and con's decided that instead of heading down the canal that day, they would go the other way into Ft. Wayne and celebrate their arrival. McQuae was the only exception. Yes, he knew that the Irish were happiest when they grouped together and shared their good times and bad times. But, for some strange reason he wanted to be alone. He had taken that first step back in Ireland that put him where he was and by all that was holy he was going to finish the journey by himself no matter where it ended.

There were still three good hours of daylight remaining as Sean McQuae headed east along the banks of the canal ditch. He had second thoughts about his decision to leave his fellow travelers and could still hear them in the distance laughing and carrying on as if they were still on a Sunday outing. But, he knew he had made the right decision. "After all," he thought, "those boys will fill themselves with spirits, loosen their tongues, eventually start talking about religion and politics, start cracking skulls, and find themselves sleeping it all off in a jail somewhere. And, if jails in America were anything like they were in Ireland, a man was a fool to get within a country mile of one." With that little bit of self assurance under his belt, McQuae picked up his pace and headed east.

It was nearly dark when he came across a shanty nestled on a little knob. A light flashed through the only window in the tiny structure and the light signaled that someone was there. That was reassuring. McQuae sensed that something was wrong, though, but the gut feelings he usually relied to warn him of big trouble weren't strong enough to raise the hackles on his back. So, he made his way toward the lights. He could feel that something strange was going on and the only way he could solve the riddle would be to knock on the door and find out. Things just weren't adding up. In New York he had been paid good silver for signing to work on the canal, had been escorted for days to this ditch arriving with a full stomach and a mouth like cotton from too much whiskey, and then assured that the canal held a top paying job for him and anyone else who would ever come along. But, where was everyone? During the three hours he had followed this ditch he had not seen another living soul other than birds and furry creatures that seemed to scurry from every bush as he clipped off mile after mile. Yes, something wasn't right.

McQuae's knock was answered by a small man who seemed worn and drawn by too many bouts with the bottle or perhaps too many bouts with ailments that are always trying to put men in their graves. He knew both looks because in Ireland dying seemed to be an everyday occurrence among the people he knew, as was drinking. The only difference was that those suffering from the poison of drink always seemed to carry a smile. And, the face he could barely see in the doorway was smiling.

"Come in my friend and sit a spell."

"I'd be obliged, thank you."

The face picked up an added glow as the stranger picked up a brand from the fire and lit his clay pipe. "What brings you to this god-forsaken part of the world?"

McQuae didn't know where to begin his story and after an uneasy moment of silence said simply, "I'm looking for a Mr. Russel."

"Well, Johnny, you've found him. What can I do for you?"

They talked well into the night and McQuae's head was spinning when their conversation ended. Yes, he had signed up to work for Russel but Russel was presently out of the canal business. He was a contractor and a good one but the canal they were sitting next to was no longer being constructed, at least for the moment. This section of canal was being built to join Ft. Wayne with the Miami-Erie in Ohio. It was Ohio's responsibility to take over the funding from the state line and right now this job just wasn't that high on Ohio's priority list. So, until Ohio decided to fulfill its part of the agreement, there wasn't any work for canal laborers. In short, McQuae was in the middle of nowhere with no work and no sign of any for quite awhile.

The next morning Russel and McQuae shared a meal and continued their conversation. No, McQuae was not under legal contract to Russel nor had he ever been. No, Russel didn't expect any work in the area for at least another year, maybe two. Yes, it would be to McQuae's benefit to move on.

"Well, Mr. McQuae," Russel smiled, "you do have a problem. But, remember, there have been hundreds like you in the past few weeks."

McQuae again felt the knot drawing tight in his belly and the realization that he was on his own in a strange land for the first time since he arrived made it even more irritating. "Do you have any suggestions, Mr. Russel?"

"Well, you do have a few choices, but you'll have to do the choosing."

"I'm aware of that but I can't decide until I know what's available."

"Some of your fellows stayed in Ft. Wayne for awhile, but the upright citizens who helped settle the community just wouldn't put up with their shenanigans and drove many of them out. Some of them moved on west but a great number moved south to Cincinnati. I understand there's a big Irish community there.

"No, Mr. Russel, I don't particularly care for the community life. If it's like Ireland, you put a great number of people in a small area, they starve, get sick, and die before their time. That's not for me."

"Another option, Mr. McQuae, is St. Marys over in Ohio. I understand they're building a high reservoir over there almost as big as the one you traveled on from Buffalo to Toledo. That means lots of digging and that means lots of man power.

"I'll be able to find work there?"

"I'd bet on it, for sure. From what I hear they have thousands working on it already and after you've been in this country for awhile you'll soon find out why they always can use a strong back."

Sean didn't understanding this last part of Russel's comment and this moment anything he couldn't understand didn't concern him. "Mr. Russel, it looks as if I'm off to St. Marys. How do I get there?"

"You could keep heading east until you run into the Miami Erie and then head south. One might even find some work on the way. But, you'd be crossing some of the most miserable country in the world and it's getting on to the hot season."

"I can take heat, Mr. Russel."

It's not the heat I'm talking about. A man just can't stay healthy in that confounded swamp during the summer. Besides that, it's too easy to get lost."

"I'd like to leave today, man. How do I get there?

"Your best bet is to go back toward Ft. Wayne until you pick up the St. Marys River. You can follow that when you feel lost but head cross country whenever possible. Why, if you followed that old twisty, turning river you'd walk a hundred miles to go fifty."

Sean shook hands with Russel, turned, and again began following the deserted canal with the morning sun warming his back. "And good luck to you, McQuae," Russel shouted. McQuae stopped, threw a wave of recognition then started walking quickly picking up his pace. "St. Marys in Ohio," he thought, "let's hope your luck is better this time McQuae."

McQuae arrived in St. Marys without too much difficulty. He had been able to take his time since he had purchased staples in Ft. Wayne before he started this leg of the journey. He had followed the river most of the way and as Russel had warned it was a twister. But, the one day he had ventured cross country, he had become totally lost and had spent the better part of that day plus part of the next before he found the river again. With that experience under his belt he decided to follow the waterway that guaranteed his arrival, eventually.

McQuae arrived at St. Marys and indeed found work at the big reservoir. He had been there for more than a year now and had worked from daylight to dark ever since. And, he was bored. He received good wages, his ration of whiskey had kept him healthy, and the extra spirits he consumed at night insured total rest. But, McQuae wasn't satisfied. He was young, true, but he was looking for something more from his life. He surely didn't want to spend the rest of it digging.

For some strange reason St. Marys didn't appeal to Sean McQuae and Sean McQuae didn't appeal to St. Marys. He had visited the town only twice during the year he worked on the east bank of the reservoir and both times the town people seemed to ignore him like they did most canalers. Of course, if they had money in their pocket merchants were more than happy to remove it, but once the money was gone so was the sociability. No, St. Marys wasn't for Sean McQuae and it was time to move on. So, McQuae quit his job.

He walked down to the feeder that would eventually supply water to the Miami-Erie when the reservoir was finished and stopped when he reached that junction. McQuae had two choices. He could head south and before too long catch a canal boat that would take him to Cincinnati or he could go north and find his way back to Toledo.

Cincinnati did not appeal to him at all from what he had been told so he turned left and walked toward St. Marys. In a short while he came across a construction gang building what appeared to be a bridge. Upon closer inspection he saw that the bridge was actually a large wooded trough that would carry water over the river that flowed beneath it. McQuae thought that the trough was a good idea and amazed himself by trying to figure out alternatives for the aqueduct.

Before long he reached the small town of St. Marys and without slowing down kept on walking. "These people have roots," he thought, "and there isn't a place for me. I'll not be on the outside looking in when everyone else is on the inside looking out. Somewhere there's a place for me and by the saints I'll find it."

He continued walking north and the mellow early summer warmth made him comfortable. He passed crews of men working on the ditch and shortly after stopping for a bite to eat came to a deep cut through the high ground. It was the largest excavation he had ever seen and McQuae figured that the boys who made this big gash in the ground had really earned their pay. He noticed a group of shanties on the edge of a small grove of trees, and since it was getting dark decided to find a place for the evening.

"The more the merrier!" they had shouted when Sean walked into the group of workers that evening and his head felt like a blister the next morning when he moved on. "Well," he thought, "no man can say that the Irish aren't strong. They work all day and still have the strength to party at night." But, McQuae wasn't feeling that way right now.

He followed the canal and keeping a quick pace found himself the next evening at another junction of the Miami-Erie, this one pointing toward the setting sun. As he surveyed the situation, he remembered Mr. Russel saying that many of his countrymen had headed west and remembering those words turned that way, walked for awhile and bedded down for the night. He was back where he started, he had no money in his pocket, and it looked as if he would have to work for awhile before he went on. But, those problems would take care of themselves and right now he needed some rest.

The next morning the sun broke through the trees far too soon and McQuae packed his bedroll and continued to walk. He was stiff and tired and found it difficult to keep moving but as the day's warmth began to develop he began to feel better. Then in the distance he heard noises, men shouting, and other sounds that told him work was being done just ahead.

"Where do I find the man in charge?" McQuae asked the first sweaty body he met.

"Just up ahead a bit," was the brisk answer. "Name's Russel," added the voice as Sean walked on. He soon found the drawn face that had sent him on his way but a year ago, and he still didn't look any healthier. True, he wasn't pale because the sun had turned his skin a bright reddish brown but his eyes looked like two slashes in an overripe tomato.

"Well bless me, if it isn't McQuae!" Russel chimed.

"Mr. Russel, I see you're back in business. Can you handle another back?"

"McQuae, my friend, I could use a hundred like you. I'm behind schedule and the summer will start laying waste to us before long."

"I'll just be working long enough to put back a bit of money," said McQuae, "then I'm going to try and find my place in the west."

"Good then, let's have a tip from the barrel and get to work. By the way, we'll be heading into swamp country tomorrow so the pay goes to $2 a day."

McQuae toasted his good luck and followed Russel to the supply shanty. He picked out a shovel that seemed to feel good in his hands and joined in the work with his assigned crew, "Ah, the luck of the Irish," thought McQuae. "Mr. Russel was a good man, at least better than most of the men he had worked for in the past, and $2 a day was double the pay he had received at the reservoir. Why, if he watched his drink, by fall he would have a decent stash for his trek west."

McQuae suddenly realized he was changing and his thinking made him feel uneasy. Just a year ago he was fancy free with his primary concerns bordering around keeping himself full of food and drink. Now, he was seriously considering saving money. "Perish the thought," he said to himself, "but I have to if I want to move on."

The days turned into weeks and as Russel had warned, the country they were now in was miserable. Much of the canal right of way was marked through swamp and instead of digging canals he found himself building canals above ground. At times he felt that the job he was doing was worth much more than his wage but the thought that it would all be over in a month or so made him stick with it. And, McQuae was taking pride in the fact that he had a growing sum of money on account with Mr. Russel.

August had turned extremely hot as was usual, but the month had also been unseasonably wet. Sickness had begun to take its toil among Russel's crew, but unlike many crews who quit work during these months, Russel had a schedule to meet. So, the work continued and those who were sick began dying.

McQuae had no idea who or how many men perished each day and it bothered him little. After all, he lived with death his whole life and took it quite matter-of-factly. As far as Sean was concerned a man started dying the minute he was born. Some just made it sooner than others.

Russel, too, tried to tone down the mortality figures that continued to rise each day. After all, he had a schedule to keep and as long as he could obtain a ready force to work he would keep on. And, keeping a steady work force was no problem because he had raised his wages to $3 per day which was far more than any other contractor had ever paid for canal labor.

McQuae continued to work and the fact that new faces kept showing up in his crew while familiar faces kept disappearing was something one didn't think about. True, men were getting sick and McQuae himself didn't feel that well. But, he was strong and luck had been riding with him ever since he left Ireland, which seemed like ages go. He was confident he could last till fall, and then he would head west and find his place to settle down.

The rains continued followed by equal amounts of scorching heat. There were few moments that Sean's body wasn't surrounded by swarming insects, and very few places on his body weren't covered with nasty colored welts. He had learned to tolerate the bugs, but now his legs had started to swell from almost constant wading through swamp water and walking was becoming difficult. Also, every cut and scratch on his body seemed to be festering with none of them healing. Then there were the leeches—six inches of ugliness that enjoyed attaching themselves to his already rotting body drawing blood he couldn't afford to lose.

Finally, McQuae could take no more. He needed a rest, just a short rest to heal his body. The sun was burning down on his back yet he shivered uncontrollably. A touch of the fever had hit him again and like in the past he would drink a quart of Russel's finest and bed down for a day until it cleaned up.

He made his way to the shanty he called home, drank from the jug that sat by his cot until it was empty, and then began sipping from another. Finally, he collapsed and began to shake violently. McQuae realized he was sick, really sick this time, but he didn't care. He was burning up now and his eyes were covered by a crimson shield. He pulled a blanket under his chin and tried to focus on a candle that stood burning on a small table across the room. At first, the flames looked so bright they felt like hot irons being driven into his eyes. Then the pain began to fade and Sean McQuae fell into a deep sleep, his last.

The next morning Russel's foreman knocked on his shanty door to make his daily report. "Mr. Russel, we lost six more men last night. McQuae was one of them. I'll have to check the pay roster to find out the other names."

"McQuae," said Russel wearily. "And, what a shame. He was a good man, better than most, and destined for a better end than this. But, more good will live and die to build this ditch and it has to be built."

"Where should be bury the dead, Mr. Russel?"

"In the bank, as usual. It's the only high ground around and those men would probably appreciate being dry for a change. And, hurry it up; we have a canal to build."

Author's Note: It always seems that history records those who eventually make a name for themselves. This may be the proper approach. Oh the other hand, during this year when we reflect on the people that made this country great, it might be appropriate to remember that there were many more people who helped to make this a great country yet never received any recognition. And, in the case of the fictional character you have just read about, thousands of these common people gave the ultimate.

True, Sean McQuae was not dedicated to making this a great country. However, he did take part, and who can say that if he had lived he might not have turned into one of those who find themselves in recorded history.

www.ingramcontent.com/pod-product-compliance
Lightning Source LLC
LaVergne TN
LVHW011239080426
835509LV00005B/555